r(

The Real Truth
Finally Revealed

Answers
to the most frequently asked questions
about Satan's deceptions and
The Real Truth of God!

Dear Stephanie,

"... and the truth shall make you free!" John 8:32

May you continue to walk in faith and in the light of the Lord!

God Bless

In God's love

Robt Russo

Very Special thanks to my Lord God and my
Lord and Savior Jesus Christ for putting me on
this amazing journey and helping me to find my
purpose in life and the true meaning of my
existence.I also want to thank everyone
that God has put in my life that has
helped me along the way.

Introduction

U nfortunately, the world as we know it is facing absolute destruction due to all the sin of mankind. If our
love and faith in God and His Son Jesus Christ is neglected
or perverted, our society falls into misery, chaos, and or tyranny. In order to reverse this neglect, we must all be very
aware that heaven and hell truly does exist, for it is written
in God's Word, the Bible. It is furthermore written that our
behavior on earth will in fact determine our eternal destiny.
Matthew 25:46 says: *"...And these will go away into everlasting punishment, but the righteous into eternal life."*

God says that we must love one another the way that He
has loved us. We need to escape the characteristics such as
pride and selfishness, and more importantly, hatred toward
other human beings, and let each of these negativities burn in
hell. Repent of your sins for in His love for us, God does not
wish to see any of His children perish into eternal damnation.

God sends out His message clearly and forewarns us of the coming end. Matthew 24:14 says: *"And this gospel of the kingdom will be preached in all the world as a witness to all the nations, and then the end will come."* Man has much to fear because God has declared that we are entering the most catastrophic time of all human history due to our continuous sinful ways. Mankind has always been determined to live life their own way, the way they see fit. As people do this, they consider themselves to be right in their decisions, because human nature is unfortunately based on pride and selfishness. God tells us in Proverbs 12:15: *"The way of a fool is right in his own eyes, but he who heeds counsel is wise."*

Now is the time God has chosen to begin revealing Himself fully to the world. We must wake up and prepare ourselves, for the Lord has been waiting very patiently and has given us more than enough time and fair warning to turn from the error of our ways of everyday life.

This is not the time to ignore God's Word. Do not choose a life that has no hope. Furthermore, do not choose an eternity of incomprehensible pain and suffering. Be wise and heed His warning. Just like the beginning Bible prophecies that have come to pass, so are now the Bible prophecies of the end of this age.

Who am I?

I am a person who truly cares for people and I have been blessed with the true meaning of life. But it does not matter who I am because it is all about our Lord and Savior Jesus Christ. I am just meant to share with you how the book came to be.

I am just an average person who has willingly and sincerely accepted Jesus Christ into my life and has asked for forgiveness of my sins. Ever since I have accepted Him and have come to repentance, I have never looked back.

Since I have prioritized Christ in my life as first and have read God's Word (the Bible), I have gained much wisdom and understanding about what is most important in life and the way we were meant to live. Since the day that I committed my life to Him and put my trust in Him, Jesus Christ has never forsaken me and has provided for me in all of my circumstances as His Word promises. As I continue to grow spiritually in Christ, He reveals to me further understanding in His Word. There is no doubt that it is because of faith that God has blessed me with true wisdom and knowledge.

I have had my share of trials and tribulations and I have overcome them by putting my trust in Christ. God has guided me with the light of His Word and His unexplainable peace and joy through very hard times. With constant prayer and perseverance in faith, I have conquered my personal demons.

My faith has also kept me balanced. Christ delights me with who I am in Him, and reminds me softly who I am not. When I suffer, I know God still loves me. When I am on top of the world, I remember that my accomplishments mean nothing in light of eternity.

Despite what some may think, Jesus Christ is real. He is not some kind of made up concept, some idea, or philosophy. He is a person that I have come to know and likewise He knows me. I know this because while He changed me from sinner to forgiven-sinner, He also realigned my motives. I still have the same character and personality, but Christ has renewed my mind and I now want to achieve His purpose.

My obsession in being the best I can be for the sake of myself is now redirected toward God's will. Now that my motives are aligned, Christ has blessed me with the life that He has intended for me, and I no longer feel or desire the need to do my own will because I have found much joy and fulfillment in His.

Jesus Christ has helped me to become a much better person and has made me the person that He wants me to be because of my faith in Him. Christ has shown me the true meaning of life and I now live everyday through faith and trust in Christ and in the glory and power of His Word.

He has opened my eyes and my heart to a whole new perspective. He has opened my eyes to the spiritual, eternal way, the way that God sees things.

I have always thought I was right in my own way, however, I have realized that I was deceiving myself. I do not have a Ph.D. in theology but one does not need that to know God. It is about having faith in God's Word and He will enlighten you with His divine truth.

The Spirit of God has filled me since I have willingly embraced Jesus and now I am able to see the truth. I am here to share it with you through this book that God has inspired me to write. I also encourage you to obtain a copy of God's Word (the Bible).

I am now a book author and screenplay writer serving God! There is much hope with having Jesus Christ in your life!

Faith is most certainly not blind. Walk by faith and not by sight! 2 Corinthians 5:7 says: *"For we walk by faith, not by sight."*

Sin and Repentance

S in is the separation from God. We have all sinned and
have fallen short of the glory of God. God the Father
sent His only Son Jesus to die for our sins. He took the punishment that we humans deserve by being crucified on the
cross. He then was buried and rose from the dead.

The good news in all of this is that we need only to come
to repentance, to recognize that we have done wrong, and to
admit we are sinners to Jesus Christ, and to only Jesus Christ,
and then ask Him for forgiveness. 1 Timothy 2:5 says: *"For
there is one God and one Mediator between God and men,
the Man Christ Jesus."*

> *"For all have sinned and fall short of the glory of God,*
> *being justified freely by His grace through*
> *the redemption that is in Christ Jesus."*
>
> *Romans 3:23-24*

By willingly and sincerely receiving and embracing Jesus Christ alone as our Lord and Savior and by repenting of our sins through Him, we will be forgiven by the grace of God and by His good grace we will be given eternal life.

Without Jesus Christ and repentance, we are destined for eternal death, and the separation from God forever.

"For the wages of sin is death, but the gift of God is eternal life in Christ Jesus our Lord."

Romans 6:23

Credits and special thanks given to

Contents

Deception

"So the great dragon was cast out, that serpent of old, called the Devil and Satan, who deceives the whole world; he was cast to the earth, and his angels were cast out with him."

Revelation 12:9

Truth

"Jesus said to him, 'I am the way, the truth, and the life. No one comes to the Father except through Me.'"

John 14:6

"If you abide in My word, you are My disciples indeed. And you shall know the truth, and the truth shall make you free."

John 8:31-32

The Real Truth Finally Revealed

Is there anyone that I can turn to that can help me with the hope that I have lost?

Of course there is! Hope comes from having faith in Jesus Christ. So do not lose hope! Sometimes it may seem as if you are alone but you are never alone. Jesus Christ is always near and He sees and feels our every tear. Psalm 145:18-19 says: *"The LORD is near to all who call upon Him, to all who call upon Him in truth. He will fulfill the desire of those who fear Him; He also will hear their cry and save them."* Jesus wants to heal you and He is waiting for you to turn to Him so He can restore your life. Jeremiah 17:7 *says: "Blessed is the man who trusts in the LORD, And whose hope is the LORD."* There is much hope and comfort when we put our trust in Jesus Christ. He will push us ahead when it would be easy to quit and He will open doors when despair closes them. Psalm 94:18-19 says: *"If I say, 'My foot slips,' Your mercy, O LORD, will hold me up. In the multitude of my anxieties within me, Your comforts delight my soul."* Even though we live in a fallen world and will experience suffering as a result, God sent His Son Jesus to overcome the sin that causes us to suffer and has given us hope through

His death and resurrection. 1 Peter 1:3 says: *"Blessed be the God and Father of our Lord Jesus Christ, who according to His abundant mercy has begotten us again to a living hope through the resurrection of Jesus Christ from the dead."* He offers us real hope even in the worst of situations. When we invite Jesus to live in us and through us, He will give us the faith and strength we need to go on." Philippians 4:13 says: *"I can do all things through Christ who strengthens me."* If you trust God even when going through times of suffering He will use it to accomplish good purposes in your life. Romans 8:28 says: *"And we know that all things work together for good to those who love God, to those who are the called according to His purpose."* We have to focus on God's promises and not our circumstances because everything is possible once we have Christ in our lives. By not having Him in our lives we are lost. Only by turning to Christ in faith, then all will be possible. Matthew 19:26 says: *"But Jesus looked at them and said to them, 'With men this is impossible, but with God all things are possible.'"*

Many are deceived by the beliefs in doing their own will and then wonder why things never go their way or why things eventually fall apart. It is not about doing our own will, we need to listen to God and let Him use us according to His purpose. Proverbs 19:20-21 says: *"Listen to counsel and receive instruction, That you may be wise in your latter days. There are many plans in a man's heart, Nevertheless the LORD's counsel—that will stand."* God is in control and He knows what is best for us. He has bigger and better plans for us than to live an unfulfilled life. By continuing on with our own dreams, ideas, and ways we are only deceiving ourselves and we will continue to suffer from all the wrong decisions we make in our lives. There is a sovereign God at work behind the scenes who is in control and His ways are perfect and just. We need to understand that and seek out His Will in order to live a joyous, productive, and prosperous life. True life is found in the Will of God. Trusting in our own ways are futile and will only lead us both physically and eternally down the path of destruction. Proverbs 28:26 says: *"He who trusts in his own heart is a fool, But whoever walks wisely will be delivered."* Jesus wants us to stop trying to control our own destiny and to let him direct our paths so we do not go down the wrong ones. He knows the beginning to the end and therefore, He knows what is going to happen if we choose a certain path, and we simply do not. So do not turn to your ways, rather trust in God and humble yourself before Him. Let Him guide your steps and use you according to His Will. James 4:10 says: *"Humble yourselves in the sight of the Lord, and He will lift you up."* We need to embrace Jesus Christ because we cannot find meaning in any way apart from Him. Put Jesus in your life first and everything else will fall into place. We will never find peace and nothing will change for the better until we have Jesus Christ in our lives. As a result, we will continue to struggle in doing things our own way. Depending and trusting in Christ will help us get through life and all our adversities. We need to let go of our own strength and resolve and not lean on our own understanding before the real power comes — Jesus Christ. Proverbs 3:5 says: *"Trust in the LORD with all your heart, And lean not on your own understanding."* By turning to God and seeking His Will, He will turn your life around and provide for all your needs. Matthew 6:33 says: *"...seek first the kingdom of God and His righteousness, and all these things shall be added to you."* When you become a true child of God, He will always be there for you. Matthew 7:7 says: *"Ask, and it will be given to you; seek, and you will find; knock, and it will be opened to you."* Once we get to the point of understanding that God will provide for us, our needs will no longer be our primary concern. If we trust God to provide for us, take care of us, and direct our paths, while we focus on keeping His law and to love one another and help others before putting ourselves first then we will be fine, because it is the way that God wants things done. Help others in need, and have faith while God is working on providing for your needs. The key to be free is not to put the focus on ourselves but we need to submissively submit ourselves to others. Galatians 6:2 says: *"Bear one another's burdens, and so fulfill the law of Christ."*

God knows our needs and He will provide in any position that we may be in — job loss, financial problems, marriage troubles, health issues, and so on. We need not to worry, because worrying tells God that we lack faith and we do not trust in Him to handle our dilemmas in life. It is very important that we see how good God is and see the genuine truth of His Word. We have God's promise to look forward to when we commit our lives to Jesus Christ. Trust God even when your life does not make sense or when something in your life is difficult to accept and understand. He will always keep His promise; He will always provide; He will always pour out His blessings upon you. You will always have hope and direction as long as you put your trust in our Lord and Savior Jesus Christ. Only by turning to Christ with faith can one hope for His mercy and intervention to receive aid. No matter your situation or the condition the world may be in that could possibly affect you in a negative way, trust in God and do not let that alarm you. When we follow the way of God and live by the gracious law and principles of His Kingdom, it will lead us to prosperous, successful, and meaningful lives, no matter what circumstance we may be in or what the world brings our way. Do not let the bad economy bring you down because it is not the world's economy that matters, it is God's economy that counts. Do not let Satan — the enemy, instill fear in your life and do not let world media frighten you with all their negativity. You must not get caught up in all of that nonsense because God supernaturally will meet all of our needs no matter the circumstance. Psalm 59:16 says: *"But I will sing of Your power; Yes, I will sing aloud of Your mercy in the morning; For You have been my defense And refuge in the day of my trouble."* Once again we have to focus on God's Word and not our own will and God will supply us with all that we need. Philippians 4:19 says: *"And my God shall supply all your need according to His riches in glory by Christ Jesus."*

Satan will always throw circumstances at us that try to overwhelm us in order to cause us to exclude God. He always tries to get us to depend on ourselves and in many situations that people may find themselves in, it is true, they rather trust in their ways to get out of it and not look to Christ and in turn they only find themselves in deeper. If there were ever a time to trust God, it is <u>NOW</u>. In these times of evil, lost hope, and great peril, do not trust in your own bank account, your job, do not trust the economy to bring you out of your situation and do not trust other people or anything else that you believe will open doors for you. Do not ever trust in anything at any time, other than the One true and living God to bring you out of every circumstance. God is the only One who can open doors for you. He will open the right doors and close the doors which need to be closed. God will make good on all His promises. Numbers 23:19 says: *"God is not a man, that He should lie."* Jesus Christ will free you from all of your agony that results in doing things your way, once you sincerely commit and surrender yourself to Him, and let Him live through you. You must let go of your own ways and live by faith in order to experience Christ's abundant life of victory and peace. Relinquish power and control over every aspect of your life to Christ and you will experience the power of supernatural living. Trust Him to lay out your paths and trust Him to turn the ugliness in your life into beauty.

Do we need to accept Jesus Christ in order to receive eternal salvation? If so, how do we accept Him in our lives?

Acts 4:12 says: *"Nor is there salvation in any other, for there is no other name under heaven given among men by which we must be saved."* 1 John 5:12 says: *"He who has the Son has life; he who does not have the Son of God does not have life."* We can only receive eternal salvation from God through Jesus Christ. The single most important thing that we can do in our life is to receive Christ and establish a personal relationship with Him. This relationship coexists when He is our personal Lord and Savior and we are His trusting follower. Only then are we considered the children of God and can receive eternal life. John 1:12-13 says: *"But as many as received Him, to them He gave the right to become children of God, to those who believe in His name: who were born, not of blood, nor of the will of the flesh, nor of the will of man, but of God."* Willingly admit to Christ that you are a sinner and ask Him for forgiveness. Invite Jesus into your life and you will receive God's awesome grace. The moment Christ is received into your life then the Spirit of God will begin working within you to renew your heart and transform your mind. Give yourself fully to God and let His Holy Spirit guide you with the intention to achieve God's purpose. God's Will should be sought out and it should be obeyed. You must first be willing to change your ways and then rely on the strength of the Holy Spirit to change you for good. It is impossible to change on your own strength. The only possible way to change is by having Christ in your life. Once you have surrendered to Christ, God will then deliver you from your sin, temptation, and addictions, and will set you free from the destructive sinning lifestyle and the will of the flesh.

To feel the fullness and glory of God we must completely give ourselves to Him and not just part of us. He wants all of us as we cannot serve two masters; it is either the flesh or the spirit. Matthew 6:24 says: *"No one can serve two masters; for either he will hate the one and love the other, or else he will be loyal to the one and despise the other. You cannot serve God and mammon (material wealth)."* Do not listen to the one who says "I believe in Christ, but you are too much!" We are either in Christ or we are not. There is absolutely no such thing as too much and you will understand that once you truly come to faith. You must fully commit to Jesus or you are truly not of the spirit but are still of this world.

Romans 8:8 says: *"So then, those who are in the flesh cannot please God."* This is the one thing that is not to be taken lightly and it is not to be a part time endeavor. You cannot be of Christ if you are enveloped in your flesh. You need to choose what team you are on. 1 Corinthians 10:21 *"You cannot drink the cup of the Lord and the cup of demons; you cannot partake of the Lord's table and of the table of demons."* Once you have given all of yourself to Him, ask Christ to faithfully help you walk in His light and to give you the strength to overcome any temptation or any addictions that you might have, because your fleshly impulses will want to arise at times. Trust in the Holy Spirit to change you as you begin your walk with Christ. Philippians 1:6 says: *"... being confident of this very thing, that He who has begun a good work in you will complete it until the day of Jesus Christ."* As you are being renewed and begin to understand the way of God, you will begin to feel spiritually fulfilled, joyous, peaceful, and enlightened with the right and perfect way to live. The things and the ways that you thought were important to you before will no longer be. Your new self will feel like God in true righteousness and holiness. You will be of the spirit and not of this world. Turn your heart toward Jesus in faith and His love will change you. He will come into your heart and make all things new. 2 Corinthians 5:17 says: *"Therefore, if anyone is in Christ, he is a new creation; old things have passed away; behold, all things have become new."* Once you have been forgiven of your sins and have committed your life to Jesus Christ, you must continue to exercise your faith in order to grow in Him and become spiritually mature and you must also exercise your faith in order to stay spiritually fulfilled. As the Holy Spirit is renewing you, you must also do your part in staying holy because faith without action is dead — it is not real faith. In order for all of that to happen, you must stay away from worldly desires and you must mediate on the Word of God continuously, and obey it. Continue to add to your faith and build yourself up and you will have no problem staying away from the pleasures of the flesh. In doing this, God will bless you and make you a blessing to others. If you do not trust Jesus Christ to be your Lord and Savior and repent of your sins, you will continue to deprive yourself of the life and the blessings that God has intended for you and most importantly deny yourself the greatest blessing of all — eternal salvation. We have everything to gain through Jesus Christ. Christ promises in Romans 4:7: *"Blessed are those whose lawless deeds are*

forgiven, And whose sins are covered." Psalm 84:12O says:
LORD Almighty, blessed is the man who trusts in you.

If you have never accepted Christ as your personal Lord
and Savior and I strongly encourage you to do so, you need
to first let God give you a spiritual rebirth by repenting of
your sins because sin separates us from God and hinders the
spirit. John 3:3 says: *Jesus answered and said to him, "Most
assuredly, I say to you, unless one is born again, he cannot
see the kingdom of God."* 1 John 1:9 says: *"If we confess
our sins, He is faithful and just to forgive us our sins and to
cleanse us from all unrighteousness."* We need a new nature
— a divine holy nature, because we cannot truly be good
due to our fleshly sinful nature and because of our fleshly
desires. Therefore, we cannot be forgiven and gain salvation, and be children of God if we desire the worldly pleasures rather than the pleasures of the spirit. Once we receive
Christ, God will forgive us of our sins and will transform us
and give us our new holy nature. We will then be Christ-like
and be children of God and will have gained everlasting life.
We will be living and enjoying the spirit filled life and no
longer of the flesh that causes us to live in sin, which leads
to hopelessness and misery and eventually eternal separation
from God. Jesus Christ did all the work on the cross and all

that you have to do to accept Christ and be forgiven is to sincerely pray a simple prayer with faith. By the good grace of God He will then forgive you and awaken you spiritually and you will be given His free gift of eternal salvation. Heaven is a holy place and we cannot enter it until we have asked Christ to cleanse us of our sins and have been given a holy nature by God through the spiritual rebirth.

Pray

Dear Heavenly Father please forgive me for I have sinned. I'm a sinner that needs salvation. I turn from my sins and my selfish ways to live my new life in Christ. Thank You for sending your Son to die on the cross for my sins. I also believe that He rose again and now He lives. I choose to have your Son, Jesus Christ to live His life in me and through me. I surrender all that I am, all that I have, and all I shall be to you, and help me to seek out Your Will. Make me the person that You always wanted me to be. Thank you for saving me. In Jesus' name I pray. Amen!

Who is Jesus Christ?

Jesus is the sinless Son of God who was born of a virgin and has come into the world as a perfect sacrifice for mankind to save us from our sins and suffering eternal death. Luke 1:30-31 says: *Then the angel said to her, "Do not be afraid, Mary, for you have found favor with God. And behold, you will conceive in your womb and bring forth a Son, and shall call His name JESUS.* To be a perfect sacrifice, He Himself must be perfect — without sin. Since our race is infected with sin, a traditional birth could not suffice. Therefore, a miraculous entrance into the world would be necessary, hence the virgin birth. God came down as man — Jesus Christ — the God-man, (better known as the Godhead or Trinity) through the birth of a virgin, and has given mankind a beautiful free gift and the greatest blessing that anyone can ever receive from God. You and I are unable on our own to comprehend the ultimate sacrifice that Christ has made on the cross so that humankind would be offered redemption. Jesus willingly took punishment and paid the penalty that He did not deserve and was crucified to save mankind from their sins. 1 Peter 2:24 says: *"…who Himself bore our sins in*

His own body on the tree, that we, having died to sins, might live for righteousness — by whose stripes you were healed."

Jesus Himself was like God in everything, but He did not think that being equal with God was something to be used for His own benefit. So He gave up His place with God and made Himself of no reputation. He was born as a man and became a servant to serve mankind. Matthew 20:28 says: *"...just as the Son of Man did not come to be served, but to serve, and to give His life a ransom for many."* Therefore, He did not live His life supernaturally but He lived the spirit life empowered by the Holy Spirit. When He was living as a man, Jesus humbled Himself and was fully obedient to God, even to the point of His death and we cannot comprehend the pain and suffering that Jesus Christ felt as He was being tormented. When He lived His life as a human, He felt pain the same way we as humans feel pain. He was beaten severely and on top of that He was also given the cruelest and most humiliating of punishments — crucifixion. To let you know how human He was when He lived as a man, days before Jesus was going to be punished He had visions of His vicious torment and death. These visions contributed to His anguish becoming very severe that He started sweating blood — a human condition called hematidrosis. Luke 22:44 says: *"...*

And being in agony, He prayed more earnestly. Then His sweat became like great drops of blood falling down to the ground." Amazingly, while Jesus was dying on the cross, He cried out to the Father in His love for us and His selflessness to forgive us even though our sins put Him on the cross to die. Luke 23:34 says: *"Father, forgive them, for they do not know what they do."* Jesus' punishment and death for mankind and His great obedience to God has earned Him the right to be highly exalted above every name. Philippians 2:9-11 says: *Therefore God also has highly exalted Him and given Him the name which is above every name, that at the name of Jesus every knee should bow, of those in heaven, and of those on earth, and of those under the earth, and that every tongue should confess that Jesus Christ is Lord, to the glory of God the Father.* When Jesus died on the cross and then rose again from the dead on the third day, He delivered us from sin and death — eternal damnation. 1 Corinthians 15:3-4 says: *"For I delivered to you first of all that which I also received: that Christ died for our sins according to the Scriptures, and that He was buried, and that He rose again the third day according to the Scriptures."* "It is finished," these are the words that Jesus uttered seconds before His death on the cross. Christ was born to die and not born to live. His purpose in life was to deliver the human race from our sins because it was the only way for our redemption. He has satisfied the wrath of God by laying down His life for us and because of this, He has provided mankind a way out from suffering that wrath. He has given us the best gift one can possibly have — eternal life, for all whomever accepts His message of salvation.

The God of judgment is the same God of mercy and grace and is equally as wonderful as His Son Jesus. John 3:16-17 says: *"For God so loved the world that He gave His only begotten Son, that whoever believes in Him should not perish but have everlasting life. For God did not send His Son into the world to condemn the world, but that the world through Him might be saved."* Everyone on earth has sinned and because of God's love for humanity, He has laid the burden and the punishment on His only Son Jesus Christ for the sins of mankind. We are now freed from the punishment of hell. Although Jesus has died on the cross for us and has cleansed us and has taken away all our sins, it does not mean that we are ultimately saved. We need to simply and sincerely accept the free gift of salvation, which by grace He has given to us.

Before Christ — in the Old Testament, people's sins were not taken away as they are now due to His death and resurrection, they were merely covered and for that to happen they were to bring a sin offering, a perfect innocent animal with no blemishes was needed to be sacrificed, whose blood was used in order to cover their sins. Leviticus 16:27 says: *"The bull for the sin offering and the goat for the sin offering, whose blood was brought in to make atonement in the Holy Place, shall be carried outside the camp. And they shall burn in the fire their skins, their flesh, and their offal."* As much as people needed to make a sacrificial sin offering to God for their sins, it was made clear that God just wanted them to be obedient to Him so they would not have to seek out a perfect animal each and every time as a sacrifice to Him for their sins. 1 Samuel 15:22 says: *"Has the LORD as great delight in burnt offerings and sacrifices, As in obeying the voice of the LORD? Behold, to obey is better than sacrifice, And to heed than the fat of rams.* To heed His warning and being obedient to His ways is what is important to Him because it will lead us into righteousness, and keep us from harm, and from harming others. Obedience to God is for our own good. God commanded these people to set aside one day a year for their sin offering, which He called "The Day of Atonement."

Leviticus 16:29-30 says: *"This shall be a statute forever for you: In the seventh month, on the tenth day of the month, you shall afflict your souls, and do no work at all, whether a native of your own country or a stranger who dwells among you. For on that day the priest shall make atonement for you, to cleanse you, that you may be clean from all your sins before the LORD.* In the Old Testament sin was only covered. In Christ our sin is taken away once and for all. The death of animals only covered sin; Christ's death took sin away forever. The Old Testament law was a way that God was forced to deal with humanity at that time based on the fact that a cross had not yet occurred. But something was missing and the nature of man was left unchanged by the animal sacrifices. The covering of sins was not enough to give a person a new heart and a transformed mind as we are now given by faith through Jesus Christ. By my experience alone I know it was Christ and not by my own strength or anything else that has truly transformed my mind and heart and has made me the person that He wanted me to be. One cannot change or be good on their own no matter how hard they try. A fuller understanding of the Old covenant will indeed make us appreciate the blessings that we have in Jesus Christ to a fuller extent and the fullness of the forgiveness that is in Him.

When Abraham and the others in the Old Testament died that had faith in God and believed in the coming Messiah — Jesus Christ, their spirits did <u>NOT</u> go to heaven because Jesus had not yet come and die for their sins. When the Old Testaments saints died, God put their souls in a waiting place awaiting final payment of sin's penalty by the promised Messiah! This holding place was called Hades and it was a place where both the saved and unsaved were sent prior to Christ's death and resurrection. Hades was separated into two compartments. Those two compartments were separated by a gulf that could not be crossed. One compartment was a place of torment, occupied by unbelievers where a rich man's spirit was sent after his physical death. The other compartment was a place of comfort referred to as "Abraham's bosom." This is where the spirits of Abraham, Moses, David, Job, Lazarus and other believers were sent prior to the resurrection of our Lord Jesus. Luke 16:19-26 says: *"There was a certain rich man who was clothed in purple and fine linen and fared sumptuously every day. But there was a certain beggar named Lazarus, full of sores, who was laid at his gate, desiring to be fed with the crumbs which fell from the rich man's table. Moreover the dogs came and licked his sores So it was that the beggar died, and was carried by the angels to Abraham's bosom. The rich man also died and was buried. And being in torments in Hades, he lifted up his eyes and saw Abraham afar off, and Lazarus in his bosom.*

"Then he cried and said, 'Father Abraham, have mercy on me, and send Lazarus that he may dip the tip of his finger in water and cool my tongue; for I am tormented in this flame.' But Abraham said, 'Son, remember that in your lifetime you received your good things, and likewise Lazarus evil things; but now he is comforted and you are tormented. And besides all this, between us and you there is a great gulf fixed, so that those who want to pass from here to you cannot, nor can those from there pass to us.'

The believers in the Old Testament could not be sent to heaven because heaven is holy grounds and their sins were not yet forgiven. As I have stated, their sins were only covered by the animal sacrifices, not taken away. When Jesus came and died on the cross and His body lay in His tomb for three days, His Spirit descended into Hades — the lower parts of the earth. The reason Jesus went there was to preach the gospel of His atoning death to the Old Testament saints who had died and had been waiting there for Him. 1 Peter 4:6

says: *"For this reason the gospel was preached also to those who are dead, that they might be judged according to men in the flesh, but live according to God in the spirit."* When Abraham, Moses, David, Job, Lazarus and all the other Old Testament saints received the gospel, they simultaneously received Jesus' atonement for their sins. At last their long wait was over. When Jesus finally ascended into heaven, He took with Him to paradise, the spirits of His beloved Old Testament saints. No believer at that time was ever let into heaven until Christ came and fulfilled the old law and took away sin forever. This provides proof that we are all in need of a Savior — Jesus Christ, and that He is the only way!

When the new covenant was established we were given God's grace. His Son Jesus Christ became the innocent sacrifice, the Lamb who was perfect with no blemishes — sinless. The perfect animals with no blemishes that were sacrificed in the Old Testament represented Jesus Christ, who would later be slain to pay the penalty for our sins. The love that God has for mankind has driven Him to come down as man — Jesus Christ to shed His blood for us and has taken away our past, present, and future sins. We are no longer merely covered but our sins are taken away forever. Jesus fulfilled the law of the old covenant and through Him we have been given grace. Because of man's continued inability to be obedient and the weakness of our flesh, Jesus' death and shedding of blood was sacrificial and necessary for our salvation. Hebrews 9:22 says: *"And according to the law almost all things are purified with blood, and without shedding of blood there is no remission."* If there was another way, there would be no need for a crucified Christ! Matthew 26:39 says: *"He went a little farther and fell on His face, and prayed, saying, "O My Father, if it is possible, let this cup pass from Me; nevertheless, not as I will, but as You will."* If there was another way to completely cleanse us of our sins God would have absolutely passed the cup from His Son Jesus. But there was no other way and Jesus obeyed and accepted the Fathers Will.

Jesus Christ is the Lamb of God who willingly sacrificed himself because of His love for mankind and took away the sins of the world and defeated death, forever! Christ has done all the work and as I have stated earlier, all that we have to do is accept the free gift of salvation by faith and live by God's Word (the Bible). When we accept Christ and the free gift of salvation we must crucify ourselves with Him and put our old-self to rest. God wants us to sacrifice our bodies — meaning putting to death our selfish desires and worldly pleasures as a living sacrifice to Him. Romans 12:1 says: *"beseech you therefore, brethren, by the mercies of God, that you present your bodies a living sacrifice, holy, acceptable to God, which is your reasonable service."* He knows that all of the worldly pleasures get us into trouble and harm us and others as well. Therefore, being obedient to God by putting away all our worldly desires would direct us away from all of the misery and destruction that we bring upon ourselves and upon others. Also recognize that once we have accepted Jesus Christ as our Lord and Savior and as a result, are now the children of the most High God, we need to remember that we can no longer do what we want to do because He has called us to be holy. 1 Peter 1:15-16 says: *"…but as He who called you is holy, you also be holy in all your conduct, because it is written, "Be holy, for I am holy."* We cannot use and abuse our body for our vain pleasures. Our body is now the temple of the Holy Spirit. It is not our own! Many of us think that our body belongs to us and we can do what we want with it. If we belong to Christ we are the children of God and we have no right to abuse or destroy our body by indulging in fleshly pleasures and things that may harm it. 1 Corinthians 6:19-20 says: *"Or do you not know that your body is the temple of the Holy Spirit who is in you, whom you have from God, and you are not your own? For you were bought at a price; therefore glorify God in your body and in your spirit, which are God's."*

When we ask Jesus Christ into our lives to be our Lord and Savior, He brings new life, light, hope, and eternal life into our lives. Where there was darkness, there is now spiritual light. Where there was death, there is now eternal life. Where we were trapped in our sins, we now have forgiveness because Jesus Christ has died for our sins. God can renew your life, heart and mind in Jesus Christ. Let Christ light up your life!

We need to realize that it is not about ourselves and that our time on earth is short. We need to have the same attitude that Jesus had and humble ourselves and walk humbly before our God. We need to let go of our pride and selfishness and acknowledge that Jesus is our Lord and Savior and obey God. In doing this, we will live peacefully and joyously even through hard times, and it will be a much better world. We will also want to put others above our own selfish desires as Christ put us above all, including to the point of sacrificing Himself for our sins.

Even though Christ knew He was going to die on the cross for our sins, He was joyous. He was to endure horrible suffering and humiliation and death, but He was filled with the love, joy and peace of God. How can this be? We think happiness comes from a good job, a nice car, a good bank account, and so on. But true and lasting joy comes from obeying God and doing His Will. Jesus knew that in doing the Will of God His Father He would save millions of people and that we could spend eternity in heaven with Him. Do you want true joy in your life? Then obey God, live by faith, and ask Christ to be your Lord and Savior in every aspect of your life. You can have God's joy even in the midst of difficult times. Suffering on this earth, however painful, is still only temporary.

I encourage all to make the effort in having a deep meaningful relationship with Jesus Christ and <u>NOT</u> ignore it or take it for granted. Jesus in His love for us made the ultimate sacrifice and has laid down His life, in order to give us eternal life. 1 John 3:16 says: *"By this we know love, because He laid down His life for us."* He could have called upon a legion of angels to save Him, and stop the suffering but He did not. His obedience to God and His love for mankind has driven Him to the hell that He did not deserve so we can have the heaven that we do not deserve. Christ's death and resurrection is the biggest blessing that He has given us and we should thank and praise Him and be eternally grateful for what He has done for us. We owe Him everything and therefore, we should be willing to face persecution, suffer, and even die for Jesus as He did for us. Many faithful followers of Christ worldwide do face persecution and death everyday because of their faith in Christ. 2 Timothy 3:12-13 says: *"Yes, and all who desire to live godly in Christ Jesus will suffer persecution. But evil men and impostors will grow worse and worse, deceiving and being deceived."* Their persecution is not an issue to them because of their strong faith. It does not stop them from turning away from Jesus and spreading the Word of God. They believe in and love Christ and if they do suffer death at the hands of their evil persecutors, they know it is eternal life that matters and they know that they will be with God the Father and Christ His Son in a perfect eternity.

Why are there so many different religions? Which is the right belief to follow so we do not suffer eternal damnation?

One of the most sinister forms of deception is found in religious practice. It has led to lawlessness, false doctrine, disobedience, and many souls have been lost because of it. Do not be blinded by religion! Satan uses the many religions as one of his deceptive strategies. There is only one way to be saved and it is not by any religion. It is only by God's Word, His promise and His love for mankind — sending His Son Jesus to be crucified, to make atonement for our sins. It is not about religion, it is about having a personal and true relationship with God the Father and His Son Jesus Christ, and there is <u>ABSOLUTELY</u> no other way to eternal salvation. 1 John 1:3 says: *"...truly our fellowship is with the Father and with His Son Jesus Christ."* <u>DO NOT</u> be deceived by the different religions, solely rely on the Bible and pray with faith to Jesus Christ for the truth. Over the years there have been many wars unnecessarily fought over religion and since God is of love, He opposes anything that has to do with religions because of the conflicts and the hostility that they create, causing us to be separated from each other and from Jesus Christ. God did not intend for us to have religion and to be separated by these many different beliefs. It is man that has divided us all and has brought conflict and confusion upon the world because of their self-imposed religions. In fact we should not be separated by all these different beliefs, cults, and false doctrine, because in truth the whole world is one in Christ. Galatians 3:28 says: *"There is neither Jew nor Greek, there is neither slave nor free, there is neither male nor female; for you are all one in Christ Jesus."* Jesus Christ has sacrificed Himself for mankind and therefore, there should be no disagreement in leadership.

There is only one faith, one belief, and one hope and believing that offers a great deal of peace and sense of security. Ephesians 4: 4-6 says: *"There is one body and one Spirit, just as you were called in one hope of your calling; one Lord, one faith, one baptism; one God and Father of all, who is above all, and through all, and in you all."* It is the only way that makes sense. Other ways that have contrary beliefs only offer emptiness, suffering, pain, despair, and eventually eternal separation from God. If you decide to follow whatever it is that pleases you or whatever religion it may be that pleases you, then sadly you will be deceived and be led onto the path of misery and eternal destruction. We need to realize the fact that there is only one God and we are all His children, we are all one and we are all the same in His eyes and we must also recognize that the only way to be brought near to God and to be saved is through Jesus Christ and the blood that he has shed for humanity. 1 Timothy 2:5 says: *"For there is one God and one Mediator between God and men, the Man Christ Jesus."* We are deeply confused concerning God's Word, His truth, and His way of life. We have all sinned and are in need of salvation and so, in order to have everlasting life, death needs to be conquered or there would be no possible way of having life after death. Jesus conquered death and therefore, through His death and resurrection He has also conquered death for mankind. It has been proven that Jesus is the only sinless innocent being that has walked the planet and therefore, the only possible One that could purify us of our sins so we can receive eternal life, and furthermore, Jesus Christ was the only One proven to ever overcome death and because of it along with the purification of our sins, we now have the chance to be raised with Him. He has given humanity an opportunity to receive everlasting life for anyone who accepts it. He has <u>MOST CERTAINLY</u> earned the right to be our Lord and Savior.

One of the most well — attested events in the ancient world is the death and resurrection of Jesus Christ. Back in His day when Jesus was confronted by religious leaders they asked Him for signs to prove if He was the promised Messiah and His answer is stated in Matthew 12:39-40 which says: *But He answered and said to them, "An evil and adulterous generation seeks after a sign, and no sign will be given to it except the sign of the prophet Jonah. For as Jonah was three days and three nights in the belly of the great fish, so will the Son of Man be three days and three nights in the heart of the earth.* John 4:48 says: *"Then Jesus said to him, "Unless you people see signs and wonders, you will by no means believe."* Jesus also constantly confronted them about their false teachings and hypocritical lifestyles. Rather than asking Christ to show you signs and immediately dismissing the fact that He exists if you do not see any signs, exactly as the religious leaders of His day did to see if He is the promised Messiah, live by faith and trust Him to open your eyes to the divine truth. You will then see signs and miracles all around you. God puts the highest priority on faith and only reacts to faith. So take Him on His Word and believe that He is who He says He is and believe that He will do what He says He will do. God searches for those who want to serve Him. If we search and pray for help with faith through Christ, God will not let us down. You should always pray to Jesus to help you earnestly search for the truth.

The world is full of false religions and false doctrine, which Jesus warns us about in the Bible and He also warns us of a global religious deception, part of which is already at work. Religious forces are now developing that will lead to a great end time religious deception. We need to put our faith in Christ so we can be armed with spiritual knowledge and as a result, we will not be deceived by ourselves, the world, and by Satan. Bible prophecy predicts a great end time false religious system — a miracle-working Antichrist and false prophet that will deceive and influence billions of people around the world.

If one desires to be saved and to be freed of all the lies and deceptions, then he or she must not trust in false religion and false doctrine and come to trust in our one true Savior — Jesus Christ. We are only forgiven by God if we repent of our sins through Christ and through Jesus is the only way that God will give us truth and eternal life. All religions contradict one another and that is the reason why all religions and paths do not lead to God. Truth does not contradict itself. God will not institute a contradictory belief system and confuse people in an attempt to get them to believe in Him. 1 Corinthians 14:33 says: *"For God is not the author of confusion but of peace."* We are living in a culture where most people believe that all religions are the same in one way or another. Furthermore, they believe that they all lead to God and that we are all going to the same place and everything is wonderful. This is a very attractive belief and it is easy to understand why so many people are attracted to this idea. By believing this way, it makes things much easier and also people are able to shy away from any confrontations. Many believe that if there are any disagreements or differences within the religions they are small and nonessential and that there is no need for concern over it. But the religions of the world overwhelmingly disagree at the most critical points. Judaism says that Jesus is not the Messiah, but Christianity says Jesus is the Messiah. Islam says that Jesus was not crucified, but Christianity says that Jesus was crucified. Hinduism says that God has been incarnate many times, but Christianity says the incarnation was unique and an unrepeatable event. Buddhism says that the world's misery will end when we do what is right, but Christianity says because we are sinners we cannot do what is right and the world's misery will end when we believe what is right. Truth is not a matter of pride it is about saving ones soul for an eternity. Either Jesus is true and all other religions are false or other religions are true and Jesus is false. There is only <u>ONE WAY</u> to God the Father. John 14:6 says: *Jesus said to him, "I am the way, the truth, and the life. No one comes to the Father except through Me.* Unfortunately, a number of people are offended by the cross because it declares that there is only one way to God.

Throughout the major world religions, religious leaders have accredited themselves as only being teachers and prophets and never claimed to be God. Only Christ has claimed to be God and having attributes belonging only to God — to be able to forgive people of their sin, free them from their habits of sin, give people a more abundant life, and give them eternal life in heaven. That is what sets Jesus Christ apart from all others. He is the clearest and most specific picture of God and He is the voice of truth. John 12:44-46 says: *Then Jesus cried out and said, "He who believes in Me, believes not in Me but in Him who sent Me. And he who sees Me sees Him who sent Me. I have come as a light into the world, that whoever believes in Me should not abide in darkness."* John 14:9 says: *"He who has seen Me has seen the Father; so how can you say, 'Show us the*

Father'?" In the Old Testament before Christ it was prophesized that He is also God. Isaiah 9:6 says: *"For unto us
a Child is born, Unto us a Son is given; And the government will be upon His shoulder. And His name will be called
Wonderful, Counselor, Mighty God, Everlasting Father,
Prince of Peace."* Although there are other religious books
that have prophecies in them, none are one hundred percent
accurate as the Bible, and none of them point to someone like
Jesus who made incredible claims and performed incredible
deeds. The evidence for the inspiration and historical trust-
worthiness of the Bible is overwhelming, while the proof for
all other religious books are lacking. Why should we trust
any other book or anyone else other than Christ? Only Jesus
has physically risen from the dead, walked on water, claimed
to be God, raised others from the dead, and performed many
other miracles. No other religious leader has died in front
of professionally trained executioners and then placed in a
guarded tomb and then rise three days later and appeared
to many people. Only in the Bible do we have the person of
Christ who said that He alone was the Way, the Truth, and
the Life. All this adds to the legitimacy and credibility of the
Bible and puts Christ above all religions and leaders.

The lineage of Jesus Christ and how He was born also provides proof that He is our Lord and Savior. There is no other religious or spiritual leader who had a lineage like that of Jesus Christ. In the New Testament the first thing that was said about Jesus' lineage is that He was the son of David and the son of Abraham. Matthew 1:1 says: *The book of the genealogy of Jesus Christ, the Son of David, the Son of Abraham.* In the Old Testament God promised King David that the Messiah and the heir to his throne would be one of his descendants, as the King eternal, the one of whom God said in 2 Samuel 7:13-14 *"He shall build a house for My name, and I will establish the throne of his kingdom forever. I will be his Father, and he shall be My son."* The New Testament shows that Jesus Christ is the rightful heir to David's throne and He will reign from the throne of David in the Millennial Kingdom after His return. Luke 1:32 says: *"He will be great, and will be called the Son of the Highest; and the Lord God will give Him the throne of His father David."* Jesus is the ultimate fulfillment of God's promise to establish David's throne forever. There are many detailed prophecies in the Old Testament concerning the coming of a Savior and a Messiah as in the above scripture Isaiah 9:6 and it was also prophesized in the old covenant that Jesus Christ would take the punishment for our sins. Isaiah 53:5 says: *"But he was pierced for our transgressions, he was crushed for our iniquities; the punishment that brought us peace was upon him, and by his wounds we are healed."*

If Jesus was not God Himself I believe that He would have never claimed to be God and put His life in jeopardy. Claiming to be God was considered blasphemy and it meant being stoned to death. John 10 31-33, 37-39 says: *Then the Jews took up stones again to stone Him. Jesus answered them, "Many good works I have shown you from My Father. For which of those works do you stone Me?" The Jews answered Him, saying, "For a good work we do not stone You, but for blasphemy, and because You, being a Man, make Yourself God." ...If I do not do the works of My Father, do not believe Me; but if I do, though you do not believe Me, believe the works, that you may know and believe that the Father is in Me, and I in Him." Therefore they sought again to seize Him, but He escaped out of their hand.* Jesus looms above and stands apart from every other figure in history.

Very importantly, I must also mention that not only is Satan behind all the religious deceptions, but we must be aware that Satan is also the source behind the occult deceptions, such as tarot cards, astrology, channeling, Ouija boards and séances. Many people look to these for insight. Millions of people dip into the dangers of the occult and seek answers from mystics, mediums, soothsayers, fortune-tellers and other dark and evil means to find their answers. These dark practices are another part of Satan's strategy of evil tricks and deceptions designed to lead us astray. Satan and his demons are real beings and they are set on our destruction.

God condemns the occult and its practices because He knows that they are demonically influenced and can harm people. They can alter and strongly influence people's lives for the worse and cause them misery. As a result, they have ruined many families that have believed and put their faith in theses dark practices. Those who follow the path of the magic arts are on the wrong path and it is a road that leads them away from God and not toward Him. All these prac-tices take people further away from their creator and will lead them in the wrong direction and in one way or another, the end will be disaster. Many citizens of ancient Ephesus who practiced the magic arts realized the foolish error of their former lives once they became faithful followers of Christ and burned their expensive books of magic.

The Bible strongly warns people not to consult mediums, spiritists, and the demons that are associated with them but to inquire of God for the truth and for their answers. Deuteronomy 18:10-12 says: *"There shall not be found among you anyone who makes his son or his daughter pass through the fire, or one who practices witchcraft, or a soothsayer, or one who interprets omens, or a sorcerer, or one who conjures spells, or a medium, or a spiritist, or one who calls up the dead. For all who do these things are an abomination to the LORD, and because of these abominations the LORD your God drives them out from before you."* If those who practice these arts have any power, beyond being great deceivers, it is not a gift from God as some falsely claim. In fact they do not ever mention a word of God in any of their gatherings. Furthermore, they have no problem emptying one's bank account. The occult is demonically influenced and these dark practices are a way of bringing evil spirits upon you and into the world. These demonic manipulators cannot predict someone's future and cannot communicate with the spirits of the deceased as they claim, but what they are doing is channeling in and communicating with demonic spirits. It is better left alone and not trust in the magic arts because not only are they great deceivers, but in many cases the occult magic and foretelling are a manifestation of demonic powers or the result of demon possession. God warns of the ultimate punishment of those who practice and follow these magic arts. However, God does have those who have real gifts of the spirit — prophets. Ephesians 4:11 says: *"...And He Himself gave some to be...prophets."* Unlike mystics, psychics and the rest of the occult, prophets have true visions that are of God and they <u>FREELY</u> give their help and do it all in the name of Jesus Christ. Prophet's are servants of God and they always give full credit to Him for any blessing that may come upon a person as a result of the prophet's help and never do they give credit to themselves.

The Bible also warns against the false predictions of astrology, which is an ancient heathen practice that also leads to tragedy and God repeatedly condemns the associated practice of worshipping the sun, moon, and stars. Our lives are not determined by the stars or movement of planets. Jeremiah 8:1-2 says: *"At that time,"* says the LORD, *"they shall bring out the bones of the kings of Judah, and the bones of its princes, and the bones of the priests, and the bones of the prophets, and the bones of the inhabitants of Jerusalem, out of their graves. They shall spread them before the sun and the moon and all the host of heaven, which they have loved and which they have served and after which they have walked, which they have sought and which they have* worshiped. *They shall not be gathered nor buried; they shall be like refuse on the face of the earth. Then death shall be chosen rather than life by all the residue of those who remain of this evil family, who remain in all the places where I have driven them," says the LORD of hosts.* We need to go directly to Christ as our only source for true answers.

It is stated in the Bible that the reason King Saul died was because he consulted a medium for guidance rather than God and therefore, without the guidance and safeguard of the Lord, the medium and his demonic influence had lead King Saul down the path of his own destruction. 1 Chronicles 10:13 says: *"So Saul died for his unfaithfulness which he had committed against the LORD, because he did not keep the word of the LORD, and also because he consulted a medium for guidance."* The Bible also states the foolishness and failures of those who claimed the ability to predict the future based on their own powers and it also states that God is the only one that can give you true answers. Daniel 2:27-28 says: *Daniel answered in the presence of the king, and said, "The secret which the king has demanded, the wise men, the astrologers, the magicians, and the soothsayers cannot declare to the king. But there is a God in heaven who reveals secrets and He has made known to King Nebuchadnezzar what will be in the latter days."* These great deceivers and spiritual guru's talk about power yet they live a powerless life themselves.

Many people are being seriously deceived and foolishly trusting in man's traditions, false doctrine and looking for help in many different ways, rather than solely trusting upon the Lord Jesus Christ to help them find their answers. 2 Timothy 4:3-4 says: *"For the time will come when they will not endure sound doctrine, but according to their own desires, because they have itching ears, they will heap up for themselves teachers; and they will turn their ears away from the truth, and be turned aside to fables."*

We must not trust in false religion, false doctrine and not put our trust in the occult or anything else, but we must come to trust in our one true Savior — Jesus Christ. Look to the Word of God (the Bible) for God's instructions for our lives. To do otherwise is to foolishly deceive yourself, or allow Satan and others to deceive you. Once again I encourage all to walk by faith and not by sight and follow the way of Christ! 2 Corinthians 5:7 says: *"For we walk by faith, not by sight."*

I believe in God but I do not believe in Satan. How can I possibly believe in him even if I wanted to?

2 Corinthians 4:3-4 says: *"But even if our gospel is veiled, it is veiled to those who are perishing, whose minds the god of this age has blinded, (Satan) who do not believe, lest the light of the gospel of the glory of Christ, who is the image of God, should shine on them."* If there is no hell and if there is no Satan, then why did Jesus Christ have to die for our sins? If you do not believe in Satan then you have not read the scriptures and therefore, you are lacking faith. Without faith, Satan will undeniably and terribly deceive you and completely have his way with you. The scriptures warn us about Satan many times in order that we do not become blind to his deceptions. If you truly believe in God and believe in His Word (the Bible) and live by faith in Christ, then you would most certainly believe in Satan and his deceptive nature and you would know that God has created Satan as well. In fact, he was closest to God until his pride and selfishness, the worst and most evil of all sins, got the best of him. Satan became too proud and ambitious when he was determined to take the throne of God

for himself. Therefore, God removed him from his position of great dignity and honor, and cast him out from heaven. Revelation 12:9 says: *"So the great dragon was cast out, that serpent of old, called the Devil and Satan, who deceives the whole world; he was cast to the earth, and his angels were cast out with him."* Satan's influence and presence on earth is evidently revealed and he is the perpetrator that has introduced sin and rebellion to the world.

A part of Satan's continuing ambition to replace God is his passionate yearning to have others worship him. Satan is extremely intelligent and powerfully deceiving. His many years in being about have given him the expertise in manipulating mankind and his unending ambition to tempt mankind makes him an expert in falsifying the truth, therefore making him come as an angel of light. 2 Corinthians 11:14 says: *"And no wonder! For Satan himself transforms himself into an angel of light."* Satan's deceptions may seem to be the truth but they are not what they seem. They are completely on the opposite end of the spectrum of what the Real Truth is, hence The Real Truth Finally Revealed. His deceiving nature although convincing to the faithless, stands in bold contrast to the truth for which Christ stands. One of Satan's most frequently employed deceptions is the misconception that good could be attained by doing wrong. More of Satan's deceptions include unbelief, worry, confusion, disobedience, rebellion, hardening of the heart, hate, bitterness, holding grudges, sowing lies, fear, lack of emotion or feeling, to accuse and slander, pride, vanity, self interest and the list goes on. Temptations and deceptions are all around us and Satan can and will use them against us. He sends lustful temptations, the biggest of all temptations through media, television, the internet, magazines, and through covetousness individuals and drowns us in sexual sin, which destroy lives and leaves married couples devastated. He and his demons for thousands of years have led mankind into every evil deed imaginable. Satan has many strategies to deceive and tempt us and he will use any circumstance to defeat us. We all know the story of Adam and Eve and how they were tempted and gave in to Satan's temptations, but many of us do not know that Jesus Christ Himself was also tempted by Satan. So what would stop him from tempting all of mankind? Satan also used the same strategies as he uses with mankind in order to get Christ to give in to him, but not once did Jesus Christ give into his deceitful ways. Luke 4:1-13 says: *Jesus, full of the Holy Spirit, returned from the Jordan and was led by the Spirit in the desert, where for forty days he was tempted by the devil. He ate nothing during those days, and at the end of them he was hungry. The devil said to him, "If you are the Son of God, tell this stone to become bread." Jesus answered, "It is written: 'Man does not live on bread alone.' " The devil led him up to a high place and showed him in an instant all the kingdoms of the world. And he said to him, "I will give you all their authority and splendor, for it has been given to me, and I can give it to anyone I want to. So if you worship me, it will all be yours." Jesus answered, "It is written: 'Worship the Lord your God and serve him only.' " The devil led him to Jerusalem and had him stand on the highest point of the temple. "If you are the Son of God," he said, "throw yourself down from here. For it is written:" 'He will command his angels concerning you to guard you carefully; they will lift you up in their hands, so that you will not strike your foot against a stone.' " Jesus answered, "It says: 'Do not put the Lord your God to the test.' " When the devil had finished all this tempting, he left him until an opportune time.*

Satan's nature is malicious. His efforts in opposing God, God's people, and God's truth are tireless. We all need to be vigilant to Satan's schemes and deceptions. Satan's advantage is based upon one being "ignorant of his devices." Only with faith in Christ and His guidance can we be aware of the methods Satan uses to lead us astray and only then will we will be able to resist him successfully! Without Christ then we are on our own and we will be deceived. There is no excuse to be ignorant to Satan's devices because the opportunity is there for us to accept Christ in our lives. 2 Corinthians 2:11 says: *"lest Satan should take advantage of us; for we are not ignorant of his devices."* We must not let temptation get the best of us or we will drown in sin. Colossians 3:5 says: *"Therefore put to death your members which are on the earth: fornication, uncleanness, passion, evil desire, and covetousness, which is idolatry."* There are many temptations and we cannot deal with them by our own strength. We need to recognize that the only way we can fight temptation is with God's strength and His strength only. Only He has the power to deliver us from Satan. Matthew 6:13 says: *"...And do not lead us into temptation, But deliver us from the evil one. For Yours is the kingdom and the power and the glory forever. Amen.*

Satan has always been opposed to mankind's best interests; he brings disorder into the physical world by afflicting human beings. At times God allows him to afflict people for purposes of correction. 1 Timothy 1:20 says: *"...of whom are*

Hymenaeus and Alexander, whom I delivered to Satan that they may learn not to blaspheme." God has full control over Satan; therefore his power is subject to God's restrictions. Satan and his demons know the scriptures very well and they know who Jesus Christ is. Luke 4:41 says: *And demons also came out of many, crying out and saying, "You are the Christ, the Son of God!" And He, rebuking them, did not allow them to speak, for they knew that He was the Christ.* And it is written that Satan will be defeated. Revelation 20:10 says: *"The devil, who deceived them, was cast into the lake of fire and brimstone where the beast and the false prophet are. And they will be tormented day and night forever and ever."* But his pride has blinded him from reality, thus believing He can still defeat God. We can see the influence of Satan because it is that same pride, which is also blinding much of mankind from the truth. Satan cannot in anyway defeat God and nor will he be able to hinder God's plan. Satan has been defeated when Christ died on the cross; this defeat is God's greatest victory. Jesus' death turned the tables on God's enemy. By willingly giving up His life as a sacrifice, Jesus took onto Himself God's judgment for our wrongdoing. If Jesus did not shed His blood and die for us and rise again, we would forever be separated from God because of our sins and suffer eternal damnation. But sin that was originated and introduced by Satan lost its power and was purified when Jesus Christ Shed His blood and took upon Himself all the sins of the world — died and then conquered death. The final victory will come when Jesus returns and casts Satan into the lake of fire, as mentioned in the above scripture — Revelation 20:10.

A number of people have a hard time admitting and believing the existence of someone as evil as Satan, but his presence and activity explain the evil and suffering in this world. The Bible makes it clear that Satan exists and that his main work is to oppose the rule of God in the affairs of man. Many wonder why God would let Satan and evil exist in His creation and the reason is because of the free will that God has given mankind. God desires to rid all evil but if He did, it would mean that we would not have free will. We would not be able to make our own choices — right or wrong. We would only be programmed to do right. It would be as if we were robots; we would be mechanical and as a result, it would not be a sincere bond between us and our creator. Had God chosen to do it this way, there would be no meaningful and true love relationships between Him and His creation. God desires a true relationship with mankind and therefore,

He wants us to willingly come to Him and love Him with our own free will that we have been given and not be forced to love Him. Unfortunately, mankind does not use their free will wisely and so, at times God also allows Satan to afflict people for purposes of correction and discipline in order that they turn from their foolish ways.

God will eventually remove all evil. Those who are willingly following Jesus are being built into God's new Kingdom. He is gathering these true followers from all around the world and forming them into His church. When God has completed this and His last true child has come to faith in Christ by their own will, Jesus will return and the reign of God will become a reality throughout God's creation. 1 Corinthians 15:24-25 says: *"Then comes the end, when He delivers the kingdom to God the Father, when He puts an end to all rule and all authority and power. For He must reign till He has put all enemies under His feet."* The curse will finally be removed. Revelation 22:3 says: *"And there shall be no more curse, but the throne of God and of the Lamb (Jesus) shall be in it, and His servants shall serve Him."*

What is Satan's biggest deception? What is the truth about hell and why would God send us there if He is a loving God?

It is imperative that we must all be aware that there truly is a heaven and hell. Matthew 25:46 says: *"...And these will go away into everlasting punishment, but the righteous into eternal life."* Hell is <u>VERY</u> real but humankind simply <u>DOES NOT</u> understand how terrible it really is. Matthew 13:50 says: *"...and cast them into the furnace of fire. There will be wailing and gnashing of teeth."* It will be an eternity with flames of unquenchable thirst and you will be very aware and very conscious of all your torment. Mark 9:43 says *"...to go to hell, into the fire that shall never be quenched.* Hell is more horrible than anyone on earth can ever imagine, therefore we must <u>NOT</u> be oblivious to it! Being condemned to hell means a person remains there forever. It is a place far worse than the most deadly, unimaginable, horrifying place on earth, and we as humans must fully consider it and not take it lightly. There is absolutely no hope when the soul dies with the body because then you are separated from the Lord forever. You will never see the light of day or the light of

God ever again. Matthew 8:12 says: *"...And cast the unprofitable servant into the outer darkness. There will be weeping and gnashing of teeth."* Along with flames of unquenchable thirst, hell is also a place of darkness. Furthermore, suffering eternal damnation is beyond our comprehension and much worse than anything that we suffer on earth!

Mankind lives by what they see and not what is unseen. So just because you cannot physically see the spiritual realm, that does not mean it does not exist. Hell is alive and well and with faith you will be able to open your spiritual eyes and not be ignorant to it. There is a spiritual war going on between the truth and deception due to Satan's ambition in trying to overthrow God by taking God's creation — mankind, away from Him. Satan uses our minds to influence and manipulate us. Ephesians 6:12 says: *"For we do not wrestle against flesh and blood, but against principalities, against powers, against the rulers of the darkness of this age, against spiritual hosts of wickedness in the heavenly places."* Satan will do anything in order to keep the Real Truth of God's Word from getting out to the world. Satan will promise us anything just to win us over and when he does not need us anymore in his scheme of things, he will throw us out like trash. He wants us to kill and do everything that is against God's Will and His righteous ways.

Satan's biggest deception is to make us believe that he does not exist and that hell is just a place on earth, so we will all continue going about our sinful ways and not worry about suffering eternally when we die. Do not believe in that deception that we are supposed to have fun and live as sinfully as we want when we are young, as the teenage years teach us, because that is entirely a misleading notion and another man-made means influenced by Satan. If you believe in that fallacy — "You're young and you only live once so go out and do what you want and enjoy yourself," then one day if you continue on fulfilling that view, you will in fact live only once and end up painfully regretting it for an eternity! God knows that trusting and following these irresponsible beliefs leads to a life of misery and consequences. It will eventually lead to a person's physical and eternal destruction. Once you are old enough to understand the gospel you need to be obedient to God because that is what will keep you from falling into the world's careless ways. If you decide not to, not only will you suffer physical consequences but you will also suffer eternal consequences and you will be held accountable for all of your foolish actions. Revelation 20:13-15 says: *"...And they were judged, each one according to his works. Then Death and Hades were cast into the lake of fire. This is the second death, And anyone not found written in the Book of Life was cast into the lake of fire."*

Satan is occupying us with our addictions, our temptations, and our everyday distractions to keep mankind from knowing God and the Real Truth. He relentlessly does this so he can bring as many souls to him as he possibly can in order to try and defeat God, because his days are short. Satan will do anything to destroy us and as a result, the immoral things in this world are rapidly becoming worse, due to the fact that he is working harder because he knows his end is near! Satan knows how to entice us and create circumstances that will keep us far away from wanting anything to do with God our Father. Revelation 12:12 says: *"Therefore rejoice, O heavens, and you who dwell in them! Woe to the inhabitants of the earth and the sea! For the devil has come down to you, having great wrath, because he knows that he has a short time."* <u>DO NOT</u> be blinded by his evil and wicked deceptions or you will without a doubt be eternally doomed. If you want life then trust and have faith in Jesus Christ and the Word of God (the Bible). If you want death then continue on ignoring God's Word and continue on with Satan's ways. Those who do not believe and lack faith in Christ and persist in trusting Satan will be destroyed by their own sins. Revelation 21:8 says: *"But the cowardly, unbelieving, abominable, murderers, sexually immoral, sorcerers, idolaters, and all liars shall have their part in the lake which burns with fire and brimstone, which is the second death."* You will be separated from God forever because of sin and you will be brutally tormented day and night in the lake of fire for an eternity.

You must understand that God does not put us in hell and destroy us; it is our own sinful ways that separate us from God and lead to our eternal death. Isaiah 59:2 says: *"But your iniquities have separated you from your God; And your sins have hidden His face from you, So that He will not hear."* Rather than asking why would God send us to hell we ought to be asking Him, why would He save any of us from going to hell? God greatly desires to save us all, but He cannot possibly help us if we do not repent of our sins and become obedient. That much understood word sin needs to find its punishment. Unfortunately, not everyone will repent and turn from their sinful ways, so hell is necessary. God will not dilute the seriousness of His law by forgiving sin without repentance. It would not be just and it would negate

His holiness. Psalm 33:5 says: *"He loves righteousness and justice; The earth is full of the goodness of the LORD."* But by the good grace of God He will forgive us and He made it very clear that the only way to reconciliation is through His Son Jesus Christ. It is the perfect satisfaction of the just demands of a just God. God has sent His only Son Jesus to die for us so we would not have to go to hell. He knows how bad hell truly is. Therefore, He wants us to accept the free gift of salvation that He has given us and for everyone to turn to Jesus Christ in repentance before it is too late. 1 Timothy 1:15 says: *"This is a faithful saying and worthy of all acceptance, that Christ Jesus came into the world to save sinners."* To put it simply, either we repent and let Jesus pay for our sins, or we pay for them ourselves in eternal torment in hell. That is the choice that we have before us!

God reaches people in many ways and gives them numerous amounts of chances to receive Christ, but they do not see it as warnings from God and they just simply ignore it. Because we have free will, it is up to us to seek out the truth and receive the free gift of salvation that God has given us. God will not force the truth on us. However, because of His good grace He also does not leave the truth hidden from anyone. Romans 10:20 says: *"I was found by those who did not seek Me; I was made manifest to those who did not ask for Me."* God makes His truth and His presence known to mankind in many ways. Through miracles, through His Word (the Bible), and through the many ministers and disciples who sincerely want to serve Him in the right and loving way, which God has personally elected to preach His Word are all examples of His presence. God provides and has provided plenty of proof of His existence including all of His creation for us to willingly respond to Him. So when it is time for our judgment, we cannot say "I did not know."

Sin separates us from God and since God is holy, all knowing, and knows what is good for us, He will not put up with sin because He knows it is unjust and harms His children. He cannot allow sin in His presence or Kingdom because of His Holiness; He cannot be friends with darkness. Do not assume He will be there for you if you keep sinning for the wages of sin without repentance is death. You are seriously mistaken if you believe that you can do all that you want, not have Christ in your life and God will automatically grant you forgiveness. He is not our servant, He is our creator. It may be pleasing to the carnal minds of mankind to imagine that they can live as sinfully as they like in this life and still be saved in the life to come, but that is far from the truth. Jesus Christ has shed His blood for mankind to cleanse us from our sin in order to bring us close to God. Due to this selfless act; He has broken down the wall of separation between God and humanity. All that we as humans have to do to cross over to the other side of the broken down wall, is to genuinely repent of our sins through the blood that Jesus has shed for us. Genuine repentance of our sins through Jesus Christ is the only way that bridges the gap between God and humanity. Ephesians 2:13-14 says: *"But now in Christ Jesus you who once were far off have been brought near by the blood of Christ. For He Himself is our peace, who has made both one, and has broken down the middle wall of separation."* Once we have sincerely admitted our sins and asked for forgiveness through Jesus Christ, God will forgive us. He will then be there for us and will be happy to serve our every need.

Where is God and why has He brought turmoil upon us? Why is He not doing anything to stop what is happening in our nation and in the world?

If our love and faith in God and His Son Jesus Christ is neglected or perverted, our society falls into misery, chaos, and or tyranny. When the world becomes corrupted with sin, people cry out, "Where is God?" Yet they refuse to take responsibility for breaking His gracious law, which was given to us for our own protection as well as to live a happy, prosperous, righteous and productive life. Unfortunately, the world is now facing absolute destruction from all the sin of mankind and all the sin of unrepentant nations. This cataclysmic event will not happen because of some random date on a Mayan calendar and by some random means, but rather because of the sinfulness and stubbornness of humanity and the unwillingness to submit to Almighty God! Isaiah 13:11 says: *"I will punish the world for its evil, And the wicked for their iniquity; I will halt the arrogance of the proud, And will lay low the haughtiness of the terrible."* Man's sin is what brings judgment and it is man's sin that has brought turmoil to this world, NOT God! Sin is the disease that is destroying this planet. Mankind has always told God to leave us alone and therefore, God has removed His Spirit from the world. We cannot reject God, and then blame Him for His absence. He has now given the human race what we have always wanted — a world without God!

God has given humanity free will and humanity has always been determined to go about life their own way. In doing this, they consider themselves to be right in their decisions because human nature is unfortunately based on pride and selfishness. Proverbs 12:15 says: *"The way of a fool is right in his own eyes."* The core of humankind possesses an innate characteristic of wickedness, which has led to much sin and corruption. Whether through greed, dishonesty and deceit, lust, theft, violence, irresponsibility, pride, ignorance and arrogance, humans have exhibited unethical acts of selfishness which have brought destruction to the world and upon themselves. Mankind has committed every sin and has been far from being righteous and far from humbling themselves before God and each other. Humans have been ruthless and uncaring to one another and to God's gracious law and sadly, will undoubtedly suffer the consequences. Romans 2:5-6 says: *"But in accordance with your hardness and your impenitent heart you are treasuring up for yourself wrath in the day of wrath and revelation of the righteous judgment of God, who 'will render to each one according to his deeds.' "*

God desires not to judge us, therefore He has been very patient with mankind and the reason why He has continuously prolonged Christ's second coming, is to give us a chance to change from the error of our ways and have a change of heart, so we do not suffer eternally in hell. 2 Peter 3:9 says: *"The Lord is not slack concerning His promise, as some count slackness, but is longsuffering toward us, not willing that any should perish but that all should come to repentance."* 2 Peter 3:3-4 says: *"knowing this first: that scoffers will come in the last days, walking according to their own lusts, and saying, "Where is the promise of His coming? For since the fathers fell asleep, all things continue as they were from the beginning of creation."* It is by God's grace that Christ has not come thus far because if He had, then much of mankind would have perished into eternal hell. God has given us more than enough time to become responsible. However, time and time again we have proved to be irresponsible and have demonstrated that the practice of God's law is greatly needed in our nation and world today. We need to come to the full understanding that without the intervention of Christ, humans can never be righteous and can never achieve greatness, responsibility and unity. John 15:5 says: *"I am the vine, you are the branches. He who abides in Me, and I in him, bears much fruit; for without me you can do nothing."* Do not believe that we are self sufficient, we are lost without Christ and mankind will continue to drive the world into the ground with their immorality. Society has created this wicked world we live in. Instead of turning to Christ for fulfillment, we turn to things as essential means to kill the pain of an empty and futile life, such as money, pornography, alcohol, drugs, and so on. There is nothing good apart from Jesus Christ and humans can never be righteous aside from Him, because without Christ we are spiritually dead and therefore, we have no way of being convicted of our sins. In addition, we will always feel empty inside. Through Christ alone can the world be changed. He can make our hearts new, which in turn will grow healing into lives around us. The earth would be a great place to live in if man would put their faith in Christ. Instead, mankind has followed their own way and has fallen under the means of Satan. They have devastated this world and therefore, have turned this world over to God's full wrath and judgment. God's wrath is real and it is mankind's sinful manner that has undeniably aroused God's righteous anger upon us.

Living without the Spirit of God and following the way of mankind has caused a great deal of moral decay of this planet. Man's immorality and misunderstanding of the right way and the wrong way to live has caused much social crisis. Man's governing of himself and this world has failed miserably. We must not be misled any longer by all the nonsense that has eaten away the heart of our nations and must stop glorifying sin. We need to understand that where there is no Christ there is no life. There is only absolute immorality and God will condemn any nation that continues down that path. When we reject Jesus Christ we do not have the Spirit of God to protect us from Satan and his influence that he has upon the world and consequently, tragedy follows. If we would live by faith through Jesus Christ we would then understand the need to fear God and we would understand the need to live in obedience to Him. Those who fear God love Him and therefore, they will respect Him and obey Him and in turn that would lead us to live righteously. He would then always be there to take care of us all. Deuteronomy 5:29 says: *"Oh, that they had such a heart in them that they would fear Me and always keep all My commandments, that it might be well with them and with their children forever!"* If we turn from our evil ways He will bring healing and life back to our land. If we obey God He will overwhelm us with blessings and if we walk in the spirit rather than the flesh, there will be no condemnation. 2 Chronicles 7:14 says: *"...if My people who are called by My name will humble themselves, and pray and seek My face, and turn from their wicked ways, then I will hear from heaven, and will forgive their sin and heal their land."* Deuteronomy 28:1-2 *says: "Now it shall come to pass, if you diligently obey the voice of the LORD your God, to observe carefully all His commandments which I command you today, that the LORD your God will set you high above all nations of the earth. And all these blessings shall come upon you and overtake you, because you obey the voice of the LORD your God."* Proverbs 8:32: *"Now therefore, listen to me, my children, for blessed are those who keep my ways."* Romans 8:1 says: *"There is therefore now no condemnation to those who are in Christ Jesus, who do not walk according to the flesh, but according to the Spirit."* Exodus 15:26 says: *"...'If you diligently heed the voice of the LORD your God and do what is right in His sight, give ear to His commandments and keep all His statutes, I will put none of the diseases on you which I have brought on the Egyptians. For I am the LORD who heals you.'"*

We need to put God back into the world and back into our constitution in order to turn things around. We must not separate God and state because we are all one under God and it is God that we have removed from our government, which is the only solid foundation of keeping our country and our world secure. We must realize that our founding fathers lived by faith and knew that God's ways were much higher than man's ways and it was God's rights that they obeyed. There was a Bible in every public office, which was required and the Bible was used to teach in schools at every level. In one of Thomas Jefferson's writings, which are inscribed on the walls of the Jefferson Memorial in the nation's capital stated, "The doctrines of Jesus are simple, and tend to all the happiness of man." Of all the systems of morality, ancient or modern which have come under my observation, none appears to me so pure as that of Jesus. "I am a real Christian, that is to say, a disciple of the doctrines of Jesus." God who gave us life gave us liberty. And can the liberties of a nation be thought secure when we have removed their only firm basis, a conviction in the minds of the people that these liberties are a gift from God? That they are not to be violated but with His wrath? Indeed I tremble for my country when I reflect that God is just, and that His justice cannot sleep forever.

At the Constitutional Convention of 1787, James Madison proposed the plan to divide the central government into three branches. He discovered this model of government from the Perfect Governor, as he read Isaiah 33:22 which says: *For the LORD is our judge, the LORD is our lawgiver, the LORD is our king; He will save us.* In 1778 James Madison wrote a letter to the General Assembly of the state of Virginia which stated: "We've staked our future on our ability to follow the Ten Commandments with all of our heart." We have staked the whole future of American civilization, not upon the power of government, far from it. We've staked the future of all our political institutions upon our capacity to sustain ourselves according to the Ten Commandments of God. On November 9, 1772 James Madison wrote a letter to William Bradford urging him to make sure of his own salvation. A watchful eye must be kept on ourselves lest, while we are building ideal monuments of renown and bliss here, we neglect to have our names enrolled in the Annals of Heaven.

Our planet is suffering the effects of grave worldly sin because of our unrighteousness and the rejection of the truth, and our continued neglect and failure to recognize that only by faith through Jesus Christ we can be made righteous and turn from our immoral ways. Deuteronomy 29:27 says: *"Then the anger of the LORD was aroused against this land, to bring on it every curse that is written in this book."* 2 Thessalonians 2:11 *"...that they all may be condemned who did not believe the truth but had pleasure in unrighteousness."* God is the answer to all our dilemmas and we should not look to anyone or anywhere else. This is not the time to ignore God's Word. This is the time to repent. Be prepared and heed His warning because He <u>WILL</u> take action. This is the time He has chosen to remove all governments, religions, and evil from society.

It is God's turn now and He is clearly forewarning us that the end will come and that He will return — the second coming of Jesus Christ. Matthew 24:14,27 says: *"And this gospel of the kingdom will be preached in all the world as a witness to all the nations, and then the end will come...For as the lightning comes from the east and flashes to the west, so also will the coming of the Son of Man be."* The Lord is going to deliver this entire world from the burdens of man's self-rule and bondage that originates from Satan. The Lord will establish His own rule over all the earth. The end of this age will be a very frightening scenario, but for the true followers of Christ they have the comfort in knowing that it is God's plan and God offers them protection from the terrible times ahead. They recognize that the coming catastrophes the Bible prophesies are actually signs of great hope. They are eagerly waiting for the coming of Jesus Christ and are overjoyed to spend eternity with Him.

The evil ways of this world will soon come to pass and God's true children can look forward to the joyous and fulfilling new world just beyond this one. By sincerely accepting and committing our lives to Christ, we will close the door on evil and we will all have the opportunity to be part of that beautiful new world.

Is God a loving God?

God loved us before we were born and nothing can separate us from His love for us. Not our sin, not any authority, not any spiritual power. God's love is great and no one can love us more. His love can always be relied upon. Romans 8:38-39 says: *"For I am persuaded that neither death nor life, nor angels nor principalities nor powers, nor things present nor things to come, nor height nor depth, nor any other created thing, shall be able to separate us from the love of God which is in Christ Jesus our Lord."* If God was not a loving God, He would not have sent His only Son Jesus Christ to die on the cross for our sins. Love is the reason why He has applied the message of salvation in our lives. He has a burning desire to seek out and save the lost and greatly rejoices when one soul comes to faith and has been saved. Luke 15:4 says: *"What man of you, having a hundred sheep, if he loses one of them, does not leave the ninety-nine in the wilderness, and go after the one which is lost until he finds it?"* Luke 19:10 says: *"...for the Son of Man has come to seek and to save that which was lost."* We did not choose Him, but He chose us and has appointed us to live a prosperous life. John 15:16 says: *"You did not choose Me, but I chose you and appointed you that you should go and bear fruit, and that your fruit should remain, that whatever you ask the Father in My name He may give you."* God does not wish to lose any of His children, not even the wicked to the ever-suffering lake of fire. The Lord's love and forgiveness is more than any human can ever comprehend. His great love for us has caused Him to exercise mercy and grace. Ephesians 2:4-7 says: *"But God, who is rich in mercy, because of His great love with which He loved us, even when we were dead in trespasses, made us alive together with Christ (by grace you have been saved), and raised us up together, and made us sit together in the heavenly places in Christ Jesus, that in the ages to come He might show the exceeding riches of His grace in His kindness toward us in Christ Jesus."* God will forgive all that will come to Him no matter what their sins may be. Even in our blindness, the Lord is faithful and gives mankind many chances to turn to Him. He waits to hear from us day and night with open arms so He can help lighten our burdens of our daily lives. It is amazing that the almighty God with such power longs to hear from us and what we have to say. God is not an angry God who is eager to punish us or use fear to get us to change. His love for us does not depend on our behavior. You cannot earn His favor or avoid His wrath through pious activities. God loves us unconditionally and completely. God loves us despite our brokenness and sins, and He is willing to meet us wherever we are in life to help us heal and grow. His love for mankind compels Him to stand strongly against sin because sin destroys His children. God is holy and pure in His essence and He loves us so much that He works tirelessly to purify our life from sin so that we can become like Him and enter the blessings of His heavenly Kingdom. God's undying love for mankind has propelled Him to come a great distance to be one of us and work His way to us through Jesus' death on the cross. God came down as man — Jesus Christ and has sacrificed Himself to pay for our sins. No matter how deeply we are immersed in sin, we never have to be trapped there, because God has broken sins power and He longs to free us from it and give us the best life possible. Most importantly He much desires to give us everlasting life. Put your faith in Christ and trust Him to turn your life around and release you from the bondage of sin.

1 Corinthians 13:13 says: *"And now abide faith, hope, love, these three; but the greatest of these is love."* Love is the most important thing to God and it is very important that we also be kind and love one another the way that God

has loved us. God mentions many times in the Bible the importance of love and how we need to love and be kind to each other and treat others like we want to be treated. Matthew 7:12 says: *"Therefore, whatever you want men to do to you, do also to them, for this is the Law and the Prophets."* If we do not love one another how else are we going defeat Satan's contagious attitude of evil and hate?! John 15:17 says: *"These things I command you, that you love one another."* Romans 12:10 says: *"Be kindly affectionate to one another with brotherly love, in honor giving preference to one another."* We must not give Satan the time of day and stop the hatred we have towards one another as well as leave our pride and selfishness, the worst of all sins to burn in hell. We must not only love the people that love us, but we must love everyone! Matthew 5:46 says: *"For if you love those who love you, what reward have you?"* God is of love and true love can only come from Him given that one has placed his or her faith in Jesus Christ. Therefore, once Christ is received in people's hearts they will know that loving one another means to turn people toward God by speaking the good news of the gospel to them. I encourage you to read the Bible and receive Christ for your sake so that you will know the truth, and also for the reason that you will have a real love for others and know that there is no truer love in loving one another than turning people toward God so they can know Him and the truth of the gospel. 1 John 4:7 says: *"Beloved, let us love one another, for love is of God; and everyone who loves is born of God and knows God."*

Why do people say we should fear God? If He is a loving God why should we fear Him?

Proverbs 1:7 says: *"The fear of the LORD is the beginning of knowledge."* God is very loving, merciful, and gracious but we need to understand that God can also be wrathful to the evil and unjust. When the Lord is feared there are absolutely no evil intentions of any nature in that person. Proverbs 8:13 says: *"The fear of the LORD is to hate evil."* Fearing the Lord will also avoid the severity of the divine punishment. As sinful people, we have every reason to fear God; it serves as part of our motivation to be reconciled with Him. Knowing the endless power of God will help us avoid sin and keep us from doing evil. Proverbs 16:6 says: *"…And by the fear of the LORD one departs from evil."* Those who are secure in a relationship with God need not be in terror; merely they should respect His authority and fear disappointing Him out of love. Those who are not secure in such a relationship need to fear what He is capable of doing when He passes judgment upon them. Ecclesiastes 8:13 says: *"But it will not be well with the wicked; nor will he prolong his days, which are as a shadow, because he does not fear before*

God." God confides in those who fear Him. Psalm 25:14-15 says: *"The secret of the LORD is with those who fear Him, And He will show them His covenant. My eyes are ever toward the LORD, For He shall pluck my feet out of the net."*

The fear of God is a result of obedience to and love of God. Those who fear God love Him and therefore, they will respect Him and obey Him. Fearing God is having great wisdom and knowledge, in turn making us live a righteous life, and keeping us from losing our soul to sin. By having faith you will fear the Lord and understand what it means to fear Him. Do not be wise in your own eyes; be wise in spiritual knowledge. Fear the Lord and in turn you will depart from sin. It will be health to your flesh, and it will mean enjoying eternal life because fearing the Lord will bring His mercy and grace upon you. Psalm 103:8-14 says: *"The LORD is merciful and gracious, Slow to anger, and abounding in mercy. He will not always strive with us, Nor will He keep His anger forever. He has not dealt with us according to our sins, Nor punished us according to our iniquities. For as the heavens are high above the earth, So great is His mercy toward those who fear Him."*

What if we have accepted Jesus and asked Him for forgiveness but there is a certain sin that we cannot control?

Psalm 130:3-4 says: *"If You, LORD, should mark iniquities, O Lord, who could stand? But there is forgiveness with You."* Psalm 103:12 says: *"As far as the east is from the west, So far has He removed our transgressions from us."* It is important to recognize that when Jesus died on the cross and you have put your trust in Him to deal with your sins, your past, present, and future sins were <u>ALL</u> dealt with. Once He shed His blood on the cross to take away all sin, this meant that every sin that was committed, is being committed, or will be committed was taken care of. When you trust in Christ for salvation, know that your sins are already paid for and God sees you as holy and perfect because you are now in Christ. Hebrews 10:10 says: *"By that will we have been sanctified through the offering of the body of Jesus Christ once for all."* Hebrews 10:12 says: *"But this Man, after He had offered one sacrifice for sins forever, sat down at the right hand of God."* One illustration is a father with his child. A child does something wrong. Does the father still love and accept the child? Absolutely!

Satan is an accuser and He will use everything against you. He will point his finger at you and tell you that God will not accept you because of your sins and He will also tell you that you are not good enough for Him. When you have accusing and negative thoughts, call Satan for what he is, call him a liar. Satan is trying to make you feel bad to the point where you really start believing that you are not good enough for God. Do not believe that and realize that God is very loving and forgiving and that you are most certainly good enough for Him. You must learn to forgive yourself or you will keep on believing that God will never forgive you. Until God has given us our new glorified bodies, we will slip from time to time. God overlooks our nonsense and sees the potential in us. God in His love and goodness does not condemn innocent human weakness in those who are truly trying to do their very best. He knows your weaknesses and is patient with you. He will bless you as you strive to obey His commandments. It is very important however, that once you have truly accepted Christ, you continually ask Him to help you walk in His light and to stay away from sin to help you strive, because sin can hinder you from growing spiritually and you may be stuck in life. There may also be consequences as a result of that sin in this life. You must focus on God and the things of the spirit, pray to Him with faith and rely on His power to give you that strength to triumph over sin. You must realize that it is impossible to be victorious over sin just with your own strength because we will fail. Such a personal victory depends on God's grace and power in our lives and our will to offer resistance to Satan's temptations. Therefore, ask God in Jesus' name to give you the power and the will to overcome sin and temptation and to lead a moral life. Ask God to reveal to you why you are struggling with that particular sin. If it is something you enjoy doing and know it is wrong, confess it to God and ask Him to give you the desire to stop. Also seek the help of fellow believers for prayer and support. Rest in Christ and trust in Him to heal you and to bear temptation as you are striving to obey His commandments. 1 Corinthians 10:13 says: *"No temptation has overtaken you except such as is common to man; but God is faithful, who will not allow you to be tempted beyond what you are able, but with the temptation will also make the way of escape, that you may be able to bear it."* Be strong in the Lord, have faith, and wait patiently on Him while He delivers you from the bondage of sin.

It is important to recognize God's gentle "tap" of conviction on our shoulder when we are repeatedly caught in a sin. This is not because He is angry with us but because He wants what is best for us and knows where the path will lead if we continue in that direction. There may be consequences as a result of our actions, but it does not mean that God loves us any less, nor does it mean that He turns His back on us. To help you overcome sin you must always avoid predicaments that you know may lead to temptation. Do not put yourself in temptations way because that is an accident waiting to happen! For example, if you have an addiction to alcohol, then do not allow yourself to go to a bar or a place where alcohol is served, because the temptation would be too great. God gives us the strength to stand against temptation but He also expects us to use common sense.

What is Judgment Day?

Judgment Day will be a day of reckoning for all people before their creator. On that day, all who are alive and all who are dead will be judged. The ones who have accepted Christ will reign forever with Him and all those who have rejected Him and have continued on with their sinful ways will be cast into the lake of fire that was prepared for the devil and his angels where they will remain forever in pain and torment. No one knows the day or the hour when Christ will make His second appearance, not even the angels in heaven, nor Christ Himself, only the Father knows and you can be sure that He will come like a thief in the night and bring sudden destruction upon many. Matthew 25:13 says: *"Watch therefore, for you know neither the day nor the hour in which the Son of Man is coming.* 1 Thessalonians 5:1-3 says: *"But concerning the times and the seasons, brethren, you have no need that I should write to you. For you yourselves know perfectly that the day of the Lord so comes as a thief in the night. For when they say, "Peace and safety!" then sudden destruction comes upon them, as labor pains upon a pregnant woman. And they shall not escape."* We do not know when that time of Jesus' second coming will be, but we can be sure that there will be a Judgment Day. John 12:48 says: *"He who rejects Me, and does not receive My words, has that which judges him — the word that I have spoken will judge him in the last day.* Be prepared for the Lord will come unexpectedly! Matthew 24:27 says: *"For as the lightning comes from the east and flashes to the west, so also will the coming of the Son of Man be.* Then the Judgment! Are you prepared? Have you accepted Christ and repented of your sins? Matthew 25:31-36 says: *"When the Son of Man comes in His glory, and all the holy angels with Him, then He will sit on the throne of His glory. All the nations will be gathered before Him, and He will separate them one from another, as a shepherd divides his sheep from the goats. And He will set the sheep on His right hand, but the goats on the left. Then the King will say to those on His right hand, 'Come, you blessed of My Father, inherit the kingdom prepared for you from the foundation of the world: for I was hungry and you gave Me food; I was thirsty and you gave Me drink; I was a stranger and you took Me in; I was naked and you clothed Me; I was sick and you visited Me; I was in prison and you came to Me.' "* Matthew 25:40 says: *"And the King will answer and say to them, 'Assuredly, I say to you, inasmuch as you did it to one of the least of these My brethren, you did it to Me.' "*

It will be the greatest day for the faithful follower. But it will be the most terrible and most horrible day for the unbeliever because they will face a holy God for their sins. The Day of Judgment the unbeliever will be found violating God's moral law. Matthew 25:41-43 says: *"Then He will also say to those on the left hand, 'Depart from Me, you cursed, into the everlasting fire prepared for the devil and his angels: for I was hungry and you gave Me no food; I was thirsty and you gave Me no drink; I was a stranger and you did not take Me in, naked and you did not clothe Me, sick and in prison and you did not visit Me.' "* Matthew 25:45-46 says: *"Then He will answer them, saying, 'Assuredly, I say to you, inasmuch as you did not do it to one of the least of these, you did not do it to Me.' And these will go away into everlasting punishment, but the righteous into eternal life."* Those people will be tormented in hell by remembering every single chance they had to repent on earth and yet they refused and that is the most frightening feeling that can ever be felt, because once in hell there is no turning back.

Christ has died to make us righteous on the Day of Judgment by shedding His blood for us and so I hope for all to come to repentance and rejoice in Jesus before it is too late. Hebrews 9:26-27 says: *"And as it is appointed for men to die once, but after this the judgment, so Christ was offered once to bear the sins of many. To those who eagerly wait for Him He will appear a second time, apart from sin, for salvation."* We do not know the hour of our death and we do not know the hour of Jesus' coming. Therefore, we need to change the way we live and live our lives as if we were going to be judged today. Life on earth is nothing more than a blink of an eye and there is no chance in eternity to ever change your destiny. James 4:14 says: *"...whereas you do not know what will happen tomorrow. For what is your life? It is even a vapor that appears for a little time and then vanishes away."* We need to stop taking life for granted and open up our eyes to the fact that we will all eventually pass from this temporal life and immediately go before God for Judgment. Due to God's love and grace, He has given us an opportunity to gain eternal life through Christ, and to be with Him in paradise forever. I hope we recognize that and do not throw that free and gracious eternal gift of salvation away. For you <u>DO NOT</u> want to be judged without genuinely having Jesus Christ in your life!

Why does God not prevent evil and not protect the innocent from violence and death they suffer that comes from the hands of the wicked?

When God came down to earth to live among us in a human body — Jesus Christ, He did not stop bad things from happening to Himself and He definitely did not deserve to have bad things happen to Him! All He ever did here was good because He sincerely had a great love for everyone! He healed people, raised the dead, forgave sins, and He still suffered severely from the worst of all punishments and died. Why do any of us deserve more than what God had during His stay on earth? Our understanding of innocent is much different than God's. We must first realize by God's standard of righteousness, the innocent and the most moral person is looked upon God as a sinner and fall short of His glory. Romans 3:23-24 says: *"...for all have sinned and fall short of the glory of God.* We are far from being worthy. Have the innocent ever not lied? Have they ever not stolen? Have they ever not had any lustful desires and acted on them? Have they ever had a true love for others as God desires? Have they ever not hated someone and cursed them instead of blessing them? Have they ever not gotten angry and had evil intentions against somebody instead of forgiving them? Have they ever not thumbed their noses at their creator and how many times have they actually even been concerned about Him? Have they ever not been self-centered and cared only for themselves and maybe a few people that are close to them, and not given any thought or concern to the rest of us that are outside of their circle? Have they freed themselves from the love of money and freed themselves from anxiously seeking after material wealth, and have they sought out spiritual wealth instead? Have any of there motives ever not been wrong? Who really is innocent? Have the innocent ever not sinned and have followed the ways of God? Of course they have sinned! These are all sins and we are all guilty of sin! 1 John 1:8 says: *"If we say that we have no sin, we deceive ourselves, and the truth is not in us."* We now need to recognize that God is not responsible for the wicked acts of men. We must also realize that He does not violate the gift of free will to humanity, even when a person's choice means others will be harmed. As I have mentioned earlier, God can prevent evil and God desires to rid all evil but if He did, it would mean that we would not have free will. We would not be able to choose right or wrong because we would only be programmed to do right. It would be as if we were robots; we would be mechanical and as a result, it would not be a sincere bond between us and our creator. Had God chosen to do it this way, there would be no meaningful and true love relationships between Him and His creation. God desires a true relationship with mankind and therefore, He wants us to willingly come to Him and love Him with our own free will that He has given us and not be forced to love Him.

We live in a world where our good and evil actions have direct consequences and indirect consequences upon us and those around us. Injustice strikes the righteous just as much as other people in our fallen world. Once again, since God loves us He has given us the gift of free will, and sometimes that results in evil. Regardless of the cause, one has the choice and the responsibility over his or her actions. Although it may seem that God does not take action, He does prevent and does restrain acts of evil. Yet even in our unworthiness, because of His love for us and His good grace, God does however make numerous exceptions and intervenes on our free will in order to help prevent harm to ourselves and others. If He had not, this world would be a great deal worse and be in absolute chaos. God has given us the ability to choose good and evil and one of the great things that God has given mankind is free will. But the gift of freedom of choice bears immense responsibility and consequences. So rather than blaming God and questioning God for why does He not prevent evil, we should be using our free will wisely and productively and should be about proclaiming the cure for evil and its consequences and make our Lord and Savior Jesus Christ known to the world! Evil is the result of what happens when one does not have Christ!

Unfortunately, there are many wicked people in this world who are willing to follow Satan, either by accident or purposely, and achieve his will, and that is the reason why we live in a fallen world, and the reason why bad things happen! 1 Timothy 5:13 says: *"For some have already turned aside after Satan."* Those who are deceived by Satan are enslaved by him. 2 Timothy 2:26 says: *"...and that they may come to their senses and escape the snare of the devil, having been taken captive by him to do his will."* Sin exists in this world and sadly it rears its ugliness against everyone. No one is excluded. Man's inhumanity towards man due to their sinful ambition in following Satan, is to blame. Sadly, much of the world lies under the influence of the evil one. Satan is the only explanation that could possibly be behind the most vicious of evil and wickedness that floods this world and is most certainly the perpetrator behind sin. And because of the free will that we have been given, mankind persists on following Satan's sinful ways instead of God's loving ways. When one does not believe and lacks faith in Jesus Christ, they are open to all of Satan's evil influences and manipulations.

Death seems major to people who only see with their physical eyes, but to the true faithful follower of Christ who sees with their spiritual eyes and lives by faith and God's promise, death and bad things are not a major issue to them, because there is a life in eternity that awaits them. Philippians 1:21 says: *"For to me, to live is Christ, and to die is gain."* The faithful followers of Christ see death as a gain and not as a loss because they have received something much better than this life — a blissful everlasting life. The reason why many of us cannot view death as a gain is because it is impossible to see it that way unless we live by faith in Christ. Many view death as an enemy, but it is far from that for those who are in Christ because our bodies are merely a temporary means to carry our soul until Christ's faithful — God's children are called home to live with Him in an amazing eternity. We must trust God in everything; He has bigger plans for us than to make us comfortable in this life. We need to accept the reality that we do not have a right to a comfortable, easy life and that we are not entitled to have everything go our way. God is more concerned about saving His children for an eternity. He is setting up His plan for eternal life and eventually we will live in that perfect eternal world, where no evil will exist, when the last of God's true children has willingly come to trust in Jesus Christ. Until then, the bad that happens in this world God will turn it around and use it to accomplish good purposes and turn it into a blessing and help save souls. We need to recognize that God never causes evil but it is mankind's free will that does, and as much as He intervenes and prevents evil, He also needs to allow it for correction and discipline so people wake up and turn from their self righteous, careless and irresponsible ways. For example, someone has found comfort in Jesus Christ and has come to repentance and has accepted Christ's free gift of salvation because someone close to them has been murdered. This incident has made this person open their eyes and turn from their sinful ways and come to faith. It may also have been the only way that this person may have ever come to Christ and been saved eternally. But it does not stop there. This person becomes a motivational speaker and an ambassador of God and will now preach

God's truth to others and talk about the consequences of sin, both physically and eternally, and it will help save a multitude of lives and souls. This is in fact a true scenario and has happened many times worldwide. As far as the person that was murdered in this example, although it is a terrible thing physically, if they have been assured eternal salvation while living on earth and have come to faith in Christ, then I am most certain that they would have absolutely not regretted leaving this world at any point of their temporary physical life to enter eternity with Christ! 2 Corinthians 5:8 says: *We are confident, yes, well pleased rather to be absent from the body and to be present with the Lord.*

Another true example would be that a woman was brutally attacked and left for dead. Her face was beyond recognition. She spent many months in a coma, but then she finally awoke. A few more months go by and many surgeries later, she is interviewed and she talks about how this experience gave her a revelation and made her come to faith. She also mentioned that before this experience had occurred, she was a self-centered and self-absorbed person and that she definitely was not the kind hearted person that she is now. Her parents were interviewed as well and they said that their daughter is a much better and humble person and she is also much happier now, than she was before the incident. This was a horrible occurrence for her physically, but most importantly it had opened up her eyes to faith, because when we die without Christ and have not realized our wrong and sinful ways, it will be eternally consequential, we will suffer far worse and it will be for an eternity. The incident and revelation made her a better person than she was before and also now her soul is saved for an eternity. Perhaps if this episode may never have happened, her self-absorbed way may never have given her another chance to come to faith. Therefore, she would not be the kind and loving person that she is today because of her new found faith and she would also eventually have lost her soul forever. God had turned something bad — the woman's attacker free willed bad choice into a blessing. She has come to faith due to the incident, therefore saving her soul and also she has now become the loving and caring person that God wanted her to be to society. In addition, her televised testimony has touched many lives and has shed light onto many others as well.

In truth, if we look at the eternal aspect of things, the bad that happens to us physically, in light of eternity may actually be a blessing in disguise. We need to look at the spiritual and the eternal perspectives and we will see that God is more concerned about saving us for an eternity, for the reason that He knows the real pain and suffering lie in eternal hell! With faith and the wisdom of God you will most definitely understand the underlying reasons!

God takes no pleasure in even seeing the death of those who are violent and immoral toward others, but rather He would want that they turn from their ways and seek to re-orient his or her life to that of love and loyalty to God and humanity. However, they will receive their punishment in due time for their unjust ways and their unrepentant hearts. God will right the wrongs you and your loved ones suffer from violence. He <u>WILL MOST CERTAINLY</u> render to each according to their deeds, whether it is in this life, eternally or both!

What is our purpose in life?
What is the meaning of our existence?

We live in a world of busy people worried about a multitude of life issues. But in the middle of all this chaos, what is really important in life? Our primary job and focus is to seek out God and the beauty of His glorious purpose. We are His dream and He wants to have a genuine relationship with all His children and wants to be involved in all our lives. He wants us to see that with Him, we can live life to the fullest and also gain life everlasting. He wants us all to call on Him and know Him personally. We were all meant to have an intimate and personal relationship with our very own creator and sit with Him in heavenly places. God has created us to have fellowship and companionship with Him but once again, because of our own free will, many of us tend to go our own way and fail to recognize the true meaning of life and sadly, we have brought grief to God and we are breaking His heart by shattering His dreams that He has for us, to live a prosperous and joyful life. He knows that our way of life leads down a dead end street and not toward prosperity and joy. He truly wants us to enjoy life to the fullest and be free, but not use our freedom to indulge in the sinful nature. Galatians 5:13 says: *"For you, brethren, have been called to liberty; only do not use liberty as an opportunity for the flesh, but through love serve one another.* God's way of life is truly blissful and fulfilling. The way we want to live life — as sinfully as we possibly can is not a means of freedom, but it is empty, futile, and unforgiving. Proverbs 13:15 says: *"...the way of the unfaithful is hard.* God knows that it if we continue down that path the consequences will be unbearable. It will not only endanger us as well as the lives of others, but sin will also cause us much pain and suffering.

Everybody has a purpose in life, but because we do not let Jesus Christ into our lives, we will never know and understand what it may be. We go about doing our own daily tasks, walk around aimlessly and pay no attention to God. We ought to seek out His purpose and let Him use us according to His will because life is found in God's Will, not ours. Instead, we are wrapped up in materialism and everyday life and we rather not make time for Him. We are deceived in believing that everything other than God is more important. We are not even concerned about Him! He is in none of our thoughts! What seems to concern us is, eating — we live to eat, rather than eat to live, sleeping, worrying about looking good, sexual behavior, taking our children to their sporting events, watching sports, listening to sports radio and glorifying our sports idols, instead of glorifying our One true idol, who is the one, who has truly made great accomplishments for mankind. We are desperate in seeking our significant other, when we should be seeking our One true companion, who is only a prayer away. We are extremely into our technologies-such as, surfing the internet, iPhones, video games, and iPods. In addition, rather than seeking God, we waste our time watching meaningless and degrading television shows because we like to enjoy watching others humiliate themselves. As long it is not us being degraded, then it is fun. It is always at the expense of others. We also go to many different parties, clubs, and bars and saturate ourselves with alcoholic beverages, and seem to be interested in nothing more than just having a good ole' time. Furthermore, we are so into our careers, jobs and dreams and we also try to find many different ways to make lots of money. Basically we strive just to meet our short term satisfaction. We live a much empty life! Even when we are bored, we still seem to keep ourselves foolishly busy trying to find things to do, rather than using that time wisely to seek God. If we sow to the worldly desires, we will then reap corruption and not gain eternal life. Galatians 6:8 says: *"For he who sows to his flesh will of the flesh reap corruption, but he who sows to the Spirit will of the Spirit reap everlasting life."* These that I have mentioned are all our modern day idols of worship; these are our God to us that we put first before our only One true God, and so we do not have time for the One true God, the only One that will provide for all our needs and get us through any situation, the only One that has given us the free gift of salvation for anyone that will accept it. We must understand that there is nothing and not any one matter that is more important and more urgent than having Christ in our lives. We need to make time for Him on a daily basis. We must examine ourselves and <u>BE WISE,</u> and weigh out our time, energy, and efforts because we idolize, make time for, and give attention to everything else but Jesus Christ. When we replace Christ for anything, including ourselves — whatever it may be that we mount on the throne of our lives, becomes an idol. Christ should be our only hero and idol and we should put Him in our lives before anything or anyone, and what we are in need of, He will give to us.

Christ is the only One that was terribly beaten and crucified to save us from our sins, so we can be righteous when it is time for us to go before God. He is the only One that can and has given us the free gift of eternal life. Unfortunately, we will never know Jesus if we let these distractions take over our lives and sadly, we will die without ever wanting anything to do with Him and then we will be separated from God forever. We have no thought for the purpose of life or the meaning of our own existence. God has bigger and better plans for us but we rather be enveloped in our own self-indulgence. If only we had the same passion for Christ as we do for the things on earth, we would be able to turn this fallen world around. We need to make time to read the Bible and seek out God's purpose. If we do not we will never experience God's help, love, joy, peace, and the blessings that He has intended for us all and we will not experience the beauty and joy of everlasting life. What we will experience is a certain and terrifying expectation of judgment and the fury of eternal hell that will consume us. There will MOST CERTAINLY be eternal ramifications for our unwise sinful actions on earth. The faithful followers of Christ do experience His awesome glory and they have the comfort in knowing that they have been assured eternal salvation. Many of us call ourselves believers but we are not living as believers. We are far from being faithful followers. Without faith in Christ and without being engaged and involved in

God's Will and being disobedient, just believing means absolutely nothing! God wants us to keep busy, but not with worldly things. He calls us to keep busy with our spiritual gifts that He has given us, and He wants them to shine so we can help save ourselves and humanity from immorality, which will eventually cause our eternal death! Whatever gifts you may have, ask Christ to show you how you can use them towards God's Will. If you are not sure of your gifts, ask Him to reveal them to you so you can use them toward His purpose. It is not about us, our future, and our children's future. It is much more than that and much bigger than any of us, and it is everlasting. It is all about the Will of God, which is to save ourselves and others from perishing eternally because what God desires is for us all to enjoy living with Him in a blissful eternity! We need to understand that our ultimate goal of this life is to get to heaven and our ways will not get us there. There is no other way to reach that goal other than through Jesus Christ!

Do not be deceived by believing that God will be there for you and that you have received eternal life, if you truly have not accepted Jesus in your life. Mankind has shown consistently that people want to be independent from God except when they get into trouble. We cannot cut the Lord out of our lives and then ask for His protection. We cannot reject Him and then blame Him for His absence. Every day, the first thing that we should do is make time and acknowledge Christ, and take a step back to consider how we are letting the deceptions of Satan run our lives. We must look beyond ourselves and not do whatever it may be that pleases our flesh. Submit to God's plan and purpose and then you can satisfy your greatest need in a way that endures. Money does not solve our problems or bring fulfillment. Nor can material items ever bring joy to us the way that the Lord can. God is forever and everything else in this world is temporal. Why follow the temporal things, when the true treasures are stored up in Jesus Christ? Nothing can ever please the flesh; the more you feed it the more it wants. The flesh will never rest and have peace. This explains why people are empty within. We were made in the image of God and therefore, a strange, painful gnawing feeling persists in the depths of a person. This inner aloneness is always present, and very few realize it is a profound yearning for God. We may not know it but in our emptiness we are searching for Christ. In His great design He intended us for His own companionship; therefore we are never complete until we find our fulfillment in Him as our constant companion. Let go of all the things of the flesh and follow Jesus Christ and you will feel a joyous fulfillment that you have never felt before. Jesus is everything and we do not need anything more. He is our pill that cures all and He is our lottery that we so much desire to win. Do not follow your dreams and the pot at the end of the rainbow because they will lead you down the wrong path; rather follow the dreams that God has for you. Do not hold onto your old ways any longer and surrender yourself fully to Christ. Do not worry if you feel that He will cramp your life style or inconvenience you. The truth is that you will enjoy Christ's life style that He has for you much more than the one you are leading now and you will at last find true meaning and fulfillment. You will never find peace and rest in your life and meaning to your existence until you have surrendered your life to our Lord and Savior. When you do so the pieces of the puzzle of your life will finally come together. You can only feel God's full experience when you act in faith and give control to Christ and trust Him with every aspect of your life. Not to mention that your stress level will be low and none and you will live a much healthier life.

If God created us is it our own fault when we sin? If it is, then why would He not have created us the way He wanted us to be?

It most certainly is our own fault when we sin because God has given us free will, and He will hold us accountable for our sins. Sin often starts innocently, at first it is just a thought, then it is acted upon, then it becomes a habit, and before you know it, you are hooked. It becomes a full blown lifestyle and it is taken further than you could have ever imagined and has led you down the wrong path and in due course, it will lead to ones self-destruction. James 1:14-15 says: *"But each one is tempted when he is drawn away by his own desires and enticed. Then, when desire has conceived, it gives birth to sin; and sin, when it is full-grown, brings forth death."* We do not stop and think twice if what we are doing is right and if our actions will harm us or others in the process, or if we even care at all. We develop tunnel vision because of our own self-interest. Therefore, we must take full responsibility for our own actions and stop blaming God for everything. Matthew 27:3-4 says: *"When Judas, who had betrayed him, saw that Jesus was condemned, he was seized with remorse and returned the thirty silver coins to the chief priests and the elders. 'I have sinned,' he said, 'for I have betrayed innocent blood.' 'What is that to us?' they replied. 'That's your responsibility.'* " Satan will tempt us in life and will go out of his way to try and make us sin. However, he cannot force us to do anything; in the end it is our own decision to follow good or evil. God created us with an inner sense of right and wrong and the ability to make our own decisions — free will, which is why it is our responsibility to choose the right direction in life. We should use the awareness He has given us wisely because there will always be consequences, if we do not. There is no excuse whatsoever for us to choose the wrong path because the Lord is there to help us make the right choices and give us the strength to endure temptation. But because of our free will we need to call on Him if we want to accept Him in our lives, not the other way around. We must decide on our own to willingly and sincerely receive Jesus and let him be our guide through life. If we do He will wipe away all our sins and He will gladly lead us through our journey. We need to learn from all our mistakes and fully submit to God. He will then condemn evil thoughts and feelings and empower us to deny temptation. We must resist the father of all lies, the greatest tempter and deceiver of mankind and with the power of God, Satan will flee from us. Our actions in life <u>WILL</u> determine our eternal destiny! When choosing your eternal destiny, I encourage you to choose wisely and to receive our true Messiah — Jesus Christ.

God wants us to love Him as much as we want to be loved but He wants us to come to Him on our own free will and our free heart that He has given us. If He created us the way that He wanted us to be — righteous, then we would not have free will and it would be as if we were forced to love Him. If He forced us to love Him then what would be the point in Him creating us?! Forced love would not be a true relationship, which God so much desires to have with mankind. If we were programmed to only do right and not have any other choices then we would be mechanical and robotic and therefore, it would not be a sincere relationship between us and God. There would absolutely be no true love, satisfaction, pleasure, and truth if we had this type of relationship with our creator.

In the Trinity are the three divine Persons really distinct from one another?

Matthew 3:16-17 says: *"When He had been baptized, Jesus came up immediately from the water; and behold, the heavens were opened to Him, and He saw the Spirit of God descending like a dove and alighting upon Him. And suddenly a voice came from heaven, saying, 'This is My beloved Son, in whom I am well pleased.'"* If they were the same, they would not appear separately as they do in Matthew 3:16-17. In spite of being different, they are "one." John 10:30 says: *"I and My Father are one."* Yet, followers of several cults are taught that Jesus is "just a prophet," or "only the Son of God" — not God Himself. This mistaken viewpoint is easily made clear by looking at 1 Timothy 3:16 which says: *"...God was manifested in the flesh (Jesus Christ)."* Also we can look at Isaiah 9:6 which says: *"For unto us a Child is born, Unto us a Son is given; And the government will be upon His shoulder. And His name will be called Wonderful, Counselor, Mighty God, Everlasting Father, Prince of Peace."* God has clearly revealed to us many times in the Scriptures that He is the One and only true God and that there are three distinctions within the One

God. The Father is God and the first Person of the Blessed Trinity. The Son is God and the second Person of the Blessed Trinity. The Holy Spirit is God and the third Person of the Blessed Trinity. This makes up the entirety of God and it is known as the Trinity or the Godhead. Colossians 2:9 says: *"For in Him dwells all the fullness of the Godhead bodily."* The term Trinity is not found in the Bible but is a theological word which expresses the clear teaching of Holy Scripture. They have three distinct personalities; each member of the Trinity has a will, can speak, can love. They are in absolute harmony consisting of one substance. They are coequal; coeternal and they are all equally as powerful. Each member is entirely God and no one member alone is the totality of God. Jesus the Son has two natures; He is truly divine — God, and truly human and His purpose to save mankind from their sins by dying on the cross and then rising again is evident. The Holy Spirit is divine in nature and He serves to convince the world of the truth concerning sin, righteousness, and judgment. The Holy Spirit is something that cannot be received or experienced by people in the world until God the Father grants them forgiveness. Once mankind has repented of their sins through Jesus Christ, God the father will then grant them forgiveness. Finally the Holy Spirit will then give mankind the ability to see the things of the spirit and open their eyes to the deceitfulness of sin. God the Father has planned a person's salvation for the ones that will want to be saved; God the Son has procured the person's salvation by His death and resurrection, and God the Holy Spirit has applied that salvation to the person's heart and life. Each member of the Trinity has a will and together they make up the totality of God.

A good analogy of the Trinity would be that water is one existing in three forms. Water can come in the form of ice, it can come in the form of liquid, and water can also come in the form of gas. The Trinity is the truth that God has revealed to us. We must firmly and faithfully believe in it. Believing in any other idea is false and is against the Word of God, and cannot result in salvation. Our understanding of God is always partial and limited; only He can know perfectly Himself. The Trinity can best be understood through enlightenment. This enlightenment is a divine revelation from the Spirit of God and it will only be given to you by opening your heart to God's Word with faith and repentance of your sins through Jesus Christ. By the grace of God, the Holy Spirit will then enlighten you with the divine truth.

What is the purpose of the Holy Spirit?

Once you have truly accepted the grace of God — Jesus Christ and have repented of your unrighteousness, you will feel the presence of the Holy Spirit alive within you. As a result, you will walk in the light and in the obedience of the Lord. Once the light of the Holy Spirit breaks through the darkness, you will be able to see the wisdom of God. The Holy Spirit will allow you to see how immoral sin really is and He will turn you from it. Titus 2:11-14 says: *"For the grace of God that brings salvation has appeared to all men, teaching us that, denying ungodliness and worldly lusts, we should live soberly, righteously, and godly in the present age, looking for the blessed hope and glorious appearing of our great God and Savior Jesus Christ, who gave Himself for us, that He might redeem us from every lawless deed and purify for Himself His own special people, zealous for good works."* Only by the repentance of our sins through Jesus Christ are we then given God's amazing Spirit. He sends us His Holy Spirit to open our spiritual eyes to our unrighteousness in order to live a moral life and therefore, saving our soul. The Holy Spirit serves to convince the world of the truth concerning sin, righteousness, and judgment. We believe we know the right way to live but without the Holy Spirit convicting us of our iniquities, we will never know the right way. Do not be deceived by believing that we can do good on our own. Only through Jesus Christ and by the work of the Holy Spirit, can our hearts change and be made right. Isaiah 64:6 says: *"But we are all like an unclean thing, And all our righteousnesses are like filthy rags; We all fade as a leaf, And our iniquities, like the wind, Have taken us away."* However, the Holy Spirit cannot do what only we can do, and that is to decide to change. It is our own decision to make. After you have made the decision to change and you have sincerely received Jesus Christ as your Lord and savior and have repented of your sins, God will begin to transform you through His Holy Spirit and you will begin to live a new life in Christ, leaving your old ways and habits behind. He will change your craving and change the way that has led you into an enslaved lifestyle. 2 Corinthians 5:17 says: *"Therefore, if anyone is in Christ, he is a new creation; old things have passed away; behold, all things have become new."* Once you have been empowered by the Holy Spirit you will have a conscience for God and a much increased capacity to cope with all the problems of life. The more you learn about and love God through His Word (the

Bible) and through prayer, as you are being renewed by the Holy Spirit to become Christ-like, the more you will understand His Will, and desire to fulfill it. Whether things are going good or bad in your life, with the awesome power of the Holy Spirit, you will feel at peace and have the strength to face anything. You will find fulfillment and the absolute true meaning of life.

God the Father speaks to us through the Holy Spirit and the Spirit is our teacher guiding us to truth. The Spirit of God provides us with joy, peace, strength, and understanding. The Spirit of God also gives us gifts for ministry and the ability to live Godly lives. The Holy Spirit helps us to pray and He gives us wisdom and revelation of God's divine truth. The Spirit gives us the boldness to step out in faith and to speak up when needed, and the boldness gives us the courage to risk ridicule and to endure the scorn. The Holy Spirit always intercedes on our behalf.

Why should we live within the limits and in the law that God sets for us?

May believe that God's law is a restriction to man-kind, but it is the utmost absolute opposite. It is by the goodness and the grace of God that we are given limits, for the reason to protect us and to live a peaceful and joyful life. God knows what sin does to His children and living without Christ and His limits endangers the life and the soul of the sinner and it also hurts others that are in evils way. Oftentimes, we resent rules because they limit what we can do. Yet we understand that without rules that define a sport, we cannot play the game let alone enjoy it. The same concept is true in life. To live and enjoy the freedoms that we have, we have to live by the rules of society. To live life to its fullest and truly enjoy it and be free, we need to understand and abide by the rules that Jesus Christ teaches us in the New Testament. God is not out to spoil our fun but instead, He has given us grace through Jesus Christ and He wants to give us the best in life. Jeremiah 29:11 says: *"For I know the thoughts that I think toward you, says the LORD, thoughts of peace and not of evil, to give you a future and a hope."* He knows that life without Jesus Christ results in anarchy and misery. God is our creator and He most definitely knows what is best for us. Isaiah 48:17 says: *"Thus says the LORD, your Redeemer, The Holy One of Israel: 'I am the LORD your God, Who teaches you to profit, Who leads you by the way you should go.' "*

In the new covenant God has justified us by His grace through faith in Christ— meaning that when we truly repent, God remembers our sins no more and by His grace we have gained eternal salvation. Living by faith in Christ will guide us and lead us onto the right path in life. In justification God treats the sinner as if they had never sinned nor been a sinner, as if they were as perfectly obedient as Christ Himself. But we must remember, even though we are forgiven by God and have been given eternal life, we may still reap the consequences of those sins that we have committed in our natural course of life. We all suffer the consequences of sin and therefore, by God's grace Christ and limits were put there before us so we can truly be free and truly enjoy the best life has to offer and will help us to consider the consequences before we make a bad choice. If you are one that may be suffering the consequences of poor choices, let the experience humble you.

Jesus Christ is the only place to have real fun and joy. You will see that if you let Him live in you and through you. Seek out Jesus Christ in prayer and in faith, humbly surrender to Him and let Him takeover your life. Let the Spirit of God renew your heart and mind.

Why does God allow suffering in our lives? Does He really care for us?

It is the sinful desires of our flesh that causes us to suffer. The truth is God would rather see us walk in His light so we would not have to suffer. But due to our disobedience, suffering is the only way that He can get through to us. Let me put the question in another way. How much suffering will we have to go through before we will begin to acknowledge the truth? How much suffering will we have to experience before we drop to our knees in repentance before God to acknowledge our pride, our stubbornness, our selfishness, our self-righteousness, and our wrong, empty, and futile ways, and to accept and obey what is true? The Lord is very compassionate and full of mercy toward those who seek His ways. Believing in His Word will bring peace, rest, joy, security, and confidence in one's life. By not believing in the Word of God (the Bible) and being disobedient and unfaithful will lead to sorrow, suffering, pain and oppression in one's life. God's Word (the Bible) is our blueprint on how to live the righteous life, therefore turning us away from sin, which causes us misery.

God cares a great deal for us and it is because of His grace and His love for mankind that He allows suffering in our lives. There are many people that would be lost in their sins and as a result, they would be on their way in suffering eternally if God had not brought some kind of tragedy in their lives to get their attention. He tries speaking to us before any pain occurs but we pay no attention to His warnings and despise His every rebuke. Therefore, suffering is the only way that many will listen and turn from their sin. Sadly, it is the moment in our affliction when many decide to turn to God. Many people will not look up to Him until He has to put them in their place, which is sad but true. If you are not willing to humble yourself, God will humble you. Luke 14:11 says: *"For whoever exalts himself will be humbled, and he who humbles himself will be exalted."* God opposes the proud but gives grace to the humble. The real suffering and tragedy of life is a person that dies on the inside while that person lives because of sin. Do not put the blame on God; we can only blame ourselves for not taking the time in getting to know Him and therefore, we do not know how to acknowledge Him. It is by God's grace that we suffer and we need to thank Him with all our hearts for our pain and consider it a blessing, because God uses suffering to shape our character, build our faith, and to redirect us away from our sin which would eventually lead to our eternal suffering. God's sufferings and sorrows is what brings repentance and salvation.

The Lord disciplines us because He loves us. He wants us to lead a moral life, which leads to true happiness but most importantly, to save our soul. God loves us too much to let us remain as we are; He wants us to trust in Him and invest in what has eternal value, because that is what matters most. We need to understand that our suffering in this life will be worth the eternal returns. So do not settle for less and invest in Jesus Christ. We can trust that God's discipline is always in our best interest. Job 5:17 says: *"Behold, happy is the man whom God corrects; Therefore do not despise the chastening of the Almighty."* It is similar to a caring human father disciplining his children. He will discipline them because he loves them. By not disciplining your own children they will only grow up to harm themselves and others and be a thorn to society. Parents must teach their children obedience and must teach them in the way of the scriptures because only through faith in Christ one may be made righteous and truly turn from their rebellion. The scriptures are profitable for rebuking, for correction, and for instruction in righteousness. Also children must honor, respect, and obey their parents in all things and it will be righteous and very pleasing to God and all will be blessed. Disobedience brings misery to the rebellious and it brings grief and dishonor to God. Not only would a parent be causing their children harm physically as well as bringing harm to society, by not disciplining them, but sadly their children will be on their way to eternal destruction. Proverbs 23:14 says: *"You shall beat him with a rod, And deliver his soul from hell."* The Lord's rod that He beats us with to deliver our soul from hell is the suffering that we need to go through in order to wake up and turn from our sin. That is God's way of disciplining His children because it is the only way that many will listen and respond to Him and in turn become obedient. God is much more concerned with the eternal life than the physical one, because He does not want any of His children to perish into eternal damnation, due to sin. He is trying to show us the need to receive Jesus Christ in order to save us for an eternity. Instead of sitting around and watching us destroy our souls, by the Lord's good grace and the love that He has for us, He will tear down our flesh in order to get us to respond, so He can save us from eternal pain and suffering. Even the most terrible misery we could experience in this world is merciful compared to what we deserve and will experience if we do not change the error of our ways. It is hard to imagine that anyone who has come to Christ as a result of their suffering, and now is in heaven instead of hell, regrets what they went through in this life. The Bible tells us in Romans 8:18: *"For I consider that the sufferings of this present time are not worthy to be compared with the glory which shall be revealed in us."* Revelation 21:4 says: *"And God will wipe away every tear from their eyes; there shall be no more death, nor sorrow, nor crying. There shall be no more pain, for the former things have passed away."*

Satan wants us to draw a conclusion about God through our temporal circumstances. We need to look through the eyes of God and must not evaluate His eternal through the world's temporal because as I already mentioned, God is eternal and is concerned about our eternity, and not the few years we have on earth that will inevitably come to pass. The glory of God that will be revealed in us is more than you can ever imagine. Why not commit your life to Jesus and let Him lead you so you can be a part of that great glory of God?!

Is faith a gift from God?

Faith is most certainly a gift from God and it is by His grace that He gives us this amazing gift, because you cannot be saved without it. However, God does not initially give anyone this saving faith, rather it is a measure of faith that He gives us and it is given to EVERYONE. Many people understand that God blesses some with it and withholds it from others but that is far from the truth and what is stated in the scriptures. This God-given initial measure of faith that is given to all of us is an amount whereby every person is without excuse for not believing in Him. Romans 12:3 says: *"...as God has dealt to each one a measure of faith."* God does not initially provide us with saving faith because of our free will. It is only given to us when we willingly take action and desire to seek Him out and want to know God. Jeremiah 29:13 says: *"...And you will seek Me and find Me, when you search for Me with all your heart."* In order to be saved we must act on our initial measure of faith by reading, listening, and trusting the gospel. If we do not desire to believe in God and be saved then we can choose to do nothing with the initial measure of faith that God has given us. Our faith or lack thereof is due to our own free will and therefore, it is our responsibility and not God's failure because He has initially given us enough faith to believe in Him. Matthew 14:31 says: *"...And immediately Jesus stretched out His hand and caught him, and said to him, "O you of little faith, why did you doubt?"* In the above scripture, Christ is expressing that we are all given faith, we just need to open our hearts and believe and not doubt. Faith will open our eyes and give us the wisdom and knowledge of God so that we can live a life of joy, peace, truth, and be eternally saved. By constantly reading, hearing, and trusting the Word of God, your faith will grow and develop.

Once you have decided to follow your faith and have willingly and sincerely accepted Christ, you will feel a spiritual war arising within you and you must realize that Satan is trying to discourage you and he will do anything to pull you away from God, and lead you back to your old ways. At first it will seem like things are entirely not going your way and at times more so than before you accepted Christ and you will not understand why this is happening to you, given that you have accepted Him. But recognize that once you accept Christ, Satan will be testing your faith in Jesus Christ and he will be working hard to dishearten you to try and take you away from your faith. But that is a good thing; it is when you are not being tested that you should be worried. Satan only challenges people who put their faith in Jesus Christ because since you have decided to live by faith, you are now a threat to Him. He is afraid of your faith. As long as you stay dead spiritually and reject the Word of God, you are not a threat to Satan.

Crisis always arises at the point of good change because of spiritual warfare. Satan does not want anything good to happen in your life; in fact he wants to destroy it. Spiritual warfare always encompasses the birth of a miracle and by accepting Christ in your life; it is the biggest miracle one can receive. Satan knows how to tear up the core of our faith. He will plant seeds of doubt in us and will have us questioning our faith. He uses our minds as a battlefield! So do not get discouraged when things are not going your way during your course in growing with Christ. Once you realize that it is Satan trying to bring you down, you will not worry, because you will know that Satan cannot defeat you. You will know that with Jesus in your life you can find comfort in Him and you will know that He will get you through any circumstance. You will go through your trials but Christ will give you the strength and the grace to get through them. Be strong in the Lord and trust in Him and His mighty power to deliver you from evil. Stay faithful to Christ no matter what you go through and He will transform you and renew your heart. Pray to Jesus to protect you with His armor and to defend you in battle so you can stand against the devil's schemes. Ask Christ to give you the strength to resist Satan's temptations. James 4:7 says: *"Therefore submit to God. Resist the devil and he will flee from you."* It is the darkness of the spiritual world that we are battling. It is the spiritual world that influences everything in this world. Ephesians 6:10-12 says: *"Finally, my brethren, be strong in the Lord and in the power of His might. Put on the whole armor of God, that you may be able to stand against the wiles of the devil. For we do not wrestle against flesh and blood, but against principalities, against powers, against the rulers of the darkness of this age, against spiritual hosts of wickedness in the heavenly places."*

DO NOT let Satan achieve victory over you and do not let man bring you down with their hopeless opinions for it is Satan talking through them trying to tear you down and defeat you. It is God's Word that matters and stands firmly. Do not listen to the unbelievers with their negative talk towards your situation whatever it may be, because they do not know God and do not know what He can do. Let God take care of all your circumstances. Real faith is trusting and acting obediently to Christ regardless of circumstances or contrary evidence. After all, if faith depended on visible evidence, it would not be faith. Hebrews 11:1 says: *"Now faith is the substance of things hoped for, the evidence of things not seen."* Hebrews 11:3 says: *"By faith we understand that the worlds were framed by the word of God, so that the things which are seen were not made of things which are visible."* Faith is about trusting Jesus Christ with your life. By reading Hebrews Chapter eleven you can see all the men and women of the Bible that had great faith. We need to know that believing and having faith are not two in the same. One can believe but not have faith and it is faith and trusting in Jesus Christ with everything in our lives, that will unleash the power of the Holy Spirit upon us and will change our lives. With faith everything is possible. Consider it a pure enjoyment whenever you do face trials of many kinds because the testing of your faith develops patience and perseverance. James 1:2-4 says: *"My brethren, count it all joy when you fall into various trials, knowing that the testing of your faith produces patience. But let patience have its perfect work, that you may be perfect and complete, lacking nothing."* Romans 5:3-4 says: *"And not only that, but we also glory in tribulations, knowing that tribulation produces perseverance; and perseverance, character; and character, hope."* God permits trials to come into your life so that you will have the chance to exercise your faith, thus becoming a strong person and a person of good character and it will also bring positive growth and spiritual maturity. Once you have realized your trial act in faith and joy and trust that God will get you through it. You will continually get a certain trial until you have gotten the point and have acted on it by faith.

Once you have genuinely received Christ you need to stand firm and ask God for patience while you are being renewed by the Holy Spirit. You also need to surround yourself with godly, sanctified people who can help you stay the course and stay away from people that will tempt you to go back to your old lifestyle. Unfortunately, some people do not stay the course in following Christ and return to their old ways. Mark 4:15-19 says: *"And these are the ones by the wayside where the word is sown. When they hear, Satan comes immediately and takes away the word that was sown in their hearts. These likewise are the ones sown on stony ground who, when they hear the word, immediately receive it with gladness; and they have no root in themselves, and so endure only for a time. Afterward, when tribulation or persecution arises for the word's sake, immediately they stumble. Now these are the ones sown among thorns; they are the ones who hear the word, and the cares of this world, the deceitfulness of riches, and the desires for other things entering in choke the word, and it becomes unfruitful."* Sadly, they get caught up in this world and believe that Christ is not for them. They believe that He is just some kind of trial offer and that there is something better, "Give this product a try for thirty days and if you are not satisfied with this special offer, we will refund your money with no questions asked." There is nothing better than having Christ in your life and there is no other way to gain eternal life and to enter the blessings of God's Kingdom. He is the only One that can and will help us get through this life if we let Him; we cannot do it on our own. Once we have truly accepted Christ then we need to commit our lives to Him and never give up on Him. Acts 11:23 says: *"When he came and had seen the grace of God, he was glad, and encouraged them all that with purpose of heart they should continue with the Lord."* We must fight the warfare and continue to keep the faith. We must stay the course and victory will most definitely be worth the price. 2 Timothy 4:7 says: *"I have fought the good fight, I have finished the race, I have kept the faith."* God has promised much joy and blessings to those who love Him and withstood the trials and tribulations of many kinds and endured the test of faith. They will receive the most vital blessing of them all — the eternal crown of life. James 1:12 says: *"Blessed is the man who endures temptation; for when he has been approved, he will receive the crown of life which the Lord has promised to those who love Him."* Revelation 2:10 says: *"Do not fear any of those things which you are about to suffer. Indeed, the devil is about to throw some of you into prison, that you may be tested, and you will have tribulation ten days. Be faithful until death, and I will give you the crown of life."* It only makes sense that we must go through much tribulation to enter the blessings of the Kingdom of God, because we must realize that we are in battle with the enemy — Satan, and he is determined to stop us. But also realize that because of the death and resurrection of Jesus Christ, we have already won the war! All that we have to do as faithful followers is to trust Christ, and continue to stay faithful.

God never promises that we will not face adversities once we have received Christ; He promises us the strength and grace we need in order to overcome those adversities. If we pray in faith and ask Him for strength and wisdom to help us overcome our trial, often He will solve the problem;

in other cases He may give us His grace, patience, and love to see the problem from a different perspective. With faith and God's strength, we never have to become disheartened or give up no matter what trials or tribulations come our way. Great strength comes from faith in God. Do not ever be discouraged; be strong, take heart, do not grow weary, and wait patiently on the Lord. You need to continue to grow in Christ and continue on with His will. You will come to see that you will achieve victory over the enemy (Satan) and you will receive the promise of God's Word. Isaiah 40:31 says: *"But those who wait on the LORD shall renew their strength; they shall mount up with wings like eagles, they shall run and not be weary, they shall walk and not faint."* Hebrews 10:35-36 says: *"Therefore do not cast away your confidence, which has great reward. For you have need of endurance, so that after you have done the will of God, you may receive the promise."*

You may also want to make sure to be a good steward and be wise with the physical blessings that God may give you for staying faithful. May you walk in the faith and the light of the Lord!

How come when I pray I feel like I am wasting my time and getting absolutely nowhere? Is prayer important?

Prayer is very important; praying with faith is what draws a person to God and it is what gives us that close personal relationship with Him. Prayer is not supplemental, it is essential; it is the bridge to the revelation of truth. A person without prayer and faith is powerless and unwise. They will gain no wisdom in the Word of God and have no spiritual knowledge in what is true. Therefore, they will be on the bridge to deception. Proverbs 24:5 says: *"A wise man is strong, yes, a man of knowledge increases strength."* The greatest and most important moments of our lives is spent on our knees in prayer to God.

To pray you must be a part of God's family by having faith in the Son of God — Jesus Christ, and have sincerely repented of your sins because sin hinders prayer. Pray to Jesus according to His Will, with faith and without doubt, and you will receive. Mark 11:24 says: *"Therefore I say to you, whatever things you ask when you pray, believe that you receive them, and you will have them."* 1 John 5:14 says: *"Now this is the confidence that we have in Him, that if we ask anything according to His will, He hears us."* Praying according to God's Will means that if it is God's desire and intention, then He will plan to bring it about for you. Ask God to show you His Will and to give you wisdom and knowledge of the truth. In doing this, He will show you your part in life. The Biblical definition of wisdom is the ability to understand God's master plan and then find our part in it so it works. As part of having wisdom you must ask God for direction and guidance in everything you do and trust in Him to lay out your paths, so that the Lord Jesus may be glorified and that you may find your part for God's purpose in life. Pray to God to give you spiritual knowledge and an eternal perspective on your life so you can pay attention to what matters most. You need to pray and ask God to fill you with His love and with His strength so you can overcome the obstacles in your life and have the love to help others overcome their obstacles. Pray for compassion and the will to spread the Word of God because it will motivate you to speak and teach, therefore bringing others to His Kingdom. Pray for the courage to step out in faith so you can tell others about Jesus Christ. God will change you and give you a desire to reach out and tell people about Christ. God will grant your prayers and joy will fill your heart as you fulfill

His command. Love your enemies and pray for those who persecute you, for God desires to save all. Pray for others to come to faith because God wants people to find salvation and enjoy eternal fellowship with Him. 1 Timothy 2:4 says: *"...who desires all men to be saved and to come to the knowledge of the truth."* Pray to the Lord to restrain Satan and his fallen angels because they will steal the seeds of the gospel that you plant. You cannot fight evil spirits with reason or flesh and blood but you can ask the Lord to fight them for you. Without the Lord's protection in your life you are leaving yourself wide open to Satan and his demonic influences. Pray for the righteous to prosper and to put them in places of influence. Pray for those in authority. Pray for world leaders and for those who give counsel to them so that they might turn to God for the right decisions, because it is their decisions that affect the world. Pray for the healing of our nations. Pray for the revival of the church and its leaders. 1 Timothy 2:1-3 says: *"Therefore I exhort first of all that supplications, prayers, intercessions, and giving of thanks be made for all men, for kings and all who are in authority, that we may lead a quiet and peaceable life in all godliness and reverence. For this is good and acceptable in the sight of God our Savior."* Pray for your needs. God wants you to make your needs known to Him because He wants to meet your every necessity. Do not pray for just your own individual needs but pray for others so God can meet there every necessity as well. Pray with a pure heart and genuine heartfelt prayers rather than worthless repetitions. Matthew 6:7 says: *"...And when you pray, do not use vain repetitions as the heathen do. For they think that they will be heard for their many words."* Join in on prayer with groups of people because that is a very effective way of praying. Matthew 18:20 says: *"For where two or three are gathered together in My name, I am there in the midst of them."* You can pray to God at any time and wherever you are and you should talk to Him multiple times a day because He loves us and He loves hearing from us. You should also express your love to Him by telling Him you love Him. Do not only pray to God during your troubled time but pray to Him twice as much during your good times and thank Him for all of His blessings that He has given you, especially sending His Son Jesus Christ to be crucified on the cross for you, giving you the best blessing of all — eternal life. Many people look for the physical blessings, which God does give, but do not fail to recognize it is the spiritual blessings given to us by God that matter that we need to be eternally grateful for.

The Bible encourages us to persevere in prayer and always be joyful and give thanks and praise to God in all circumstances, because that is what He desires from us so our spirit will continue to have that fire to carry on. 1 Thessalonians 5:16-19 says: *"Rejoice always, pray without ceasing, in everything give thanks; for this is the will of God in Christ Jesus for you. Do not put out the Spirit's fire."* Persevering in prayer means to keep on praying and do not give up just because you do not see your prayers being answered right away. When you ask and you do not receive, it is because you may be praying with wrong and selfish motives and not praying according to God's Will. James 4:3 says: *"You ask and do not receive, because you ask amiss, that you may spend it on your pleasures."* God answers prayers but sometimes the answer is no! God may not give you certain things that you ask for because He knows that it is not right for you or you do not need it, and that it may lead to trouble and may also redirect you from what He has called you to do. You must also know that God's timing is always perfect, but because of our impatience we do not think so. We can trust that God's timing is always in our best interest. True genuine prayer of a righteous person is very powerful and effective and is the answer to all of our problems. James 5:16

says: *"Confess your trespasses to one another, and pray for one another, that you may be healed. The effective, fervent prayer of a righteous man avails much."*

Pray that God's Will be accomplished and not our own. He sincerely wants to answer our prayers and He is pleased to use the prayers of His people to accomplish His purposes in this world. God has no favorites but He helps and uses those who obey Him and want to accomplish His Will. Realize that God has better plans for you. Ask God to show you how you can use your God-given gifts toward His Will. When you let go of your own dreams and agendas and pursue God's dreams you can move forward to true greatness because He will transform you into a person with strong character like His Son Jesus Christ. Pray for the humility and humbleness that you need to give up your own dreams and agendas and follow the plans that God has for your life. You will feel much more alive when you begin to fulfill the dreams that God has intended for you. He loves us more than anything and He knows what is best for us. You can trust Him that He will bring to pass in your life what is best for you when you commit your life to Jesus Christ. But you need to continue having faith and patience, and do not give up. Pray with a clear heart, a clear mind, and pure motives. Do not do all the talking but listen to God as well. Visualize the finished product with faith and thank Him even before it has come to pass and He will show you it. Keep fully trusting God and you will see that He will bring great things into your life. I encourage you to take the time each day with God in prayer and in the study of God's Word (the Bible). When you pray, remember to pray in the name of Jesus Christ! Colossians 3:17 says: *"...And whatever you do in word or deed, do all in the name of the Lord Jesus, giving thanks to God the Father through Him.*

How come I have noticed that the wicked and or the self-righteous live a prosperous life more so than a follower of Christ?

First I would like to address that wickedness, self-righteousness, and immorality in the eyes of God are all one in the same. These ways are all prideful and evil and they will eventually lead to ones self-destruction. We need to understand that God defines prosperity much differently than the world does. The way to achieve true prosperity is by serving other people for God's glory. From God's point of view a prosperous person focuses on giving, not receiving. Recognize that true prosperity is being righteous in the eyes of God and living of the spirit, not being rich in material belongings and living of the flesh. It does not matter how prosperous we are by earthly and temporal standards, because if we are poor in spirit and lack Christ we have absolutely nothing. Unfortunately the wicked, immoral and others that trust in their self-righteous ways do not see it that way. Sadly, their lives and souls are headed for an unfortunate end. God is long-suffering and will always condemn wickedness and self-righteousness, but He will do it in His own time and His own way. He is gracious and merciful and does not take pleasure in seeing the immoral destroyed and so He will give them a chance to repent. Some of them may prosper and fare well in this world and it may seem to you more so than the faithful followers of Jesus Christ. They may live out their days in good health, success and prosperity, but what good is it if they are not right with God? Their final destination is the lake of fire and eternal destruction if they do not change the error of their ways. Mark 8:36 says: *"For what will it profit a man if he gains the whole world, and loses his own soul?"*

You also need to understand that when the wicked become an instrument in the hands of Satan to hinder or oppose the Kingdom of God and His Will, they are subject to be judged and cut off before their time. Continuous sinning and disobedience to God not only leads to eternal death, but it can also result in suffering and in an untimely physical death. If people continue on with sin and rebellion and do not produce Godly fruit, God will let Satan remove them from this world. God knows the beginning to the end and therefore, He knows the ones that will never come to the truth and never produce fruit in fulfilling God's will to help save humanity. As a result, He will have no use for them and may eliminate them before their time. The wicked choose to disregard the warning signs of danger that God graciously presents to them and continuously take on the path of self-destruction as well as the devastation of others. They act out solely to obtain pleasure or to intentionally cause harm and God may remove them before their time in order to look out for others that are around them. Obedience to God can defer death and save the life as well as the soul. There is absolutely no advantage in being wicked and self righteous.

They have their minds set on the things of this world rather than the Will of God. They are blinded by the extreme hunger to acquire earthly possessions. They are tempted and corrupted by their own greedy desires, the lust in their eyes and the blindness of their hearts misleads them and they are enticed and dragged away. They become slaves to their own evil ways. Ephesians 4:18-19 says: "...*having their understanding darkened, being alienated from the life of God, because of the ignorance that is in them, because of the blindness of their heart; who, being past feeling, have given themselves over to lewdness, to work all uncleanness with greediness.*" They replace God for things of this world and rather worship money, materialism, drugs, alcohol, sexual immortality, their systems, principles, formulas, and so on and entirely put their trust in themselves, rather than Christ. Romans 1:25 says: *"...who exchanged the truth of God for the lie, and worshiped and served the creature rather than the Creator, who is blessed forever."* They trust the things of the flesh, rather than the things of the spirit, and by obtaining worldly pleasures they are deceiving themselves. Job 15:31 says: *"Let him not trust in futile things, deceiving himself, for futility will be his reward."* The faithful in Christ must step up and pray for these lost souls and be their light and hope that they will see the error of their ways and turn from them. This will help stop the harm that the immoral are causing to themselves and the harm they are causing to society as well.

By far the morally wrong are missing the whole point of living. They live to gain everything in this life and unfortunately they give no thought to the after life. As a consequence, they will ultimately lose their soul forever because of their immorality. Psalm 1:6 says: *"For the LORD knows the way of the righteous, but the way of the ungodly shall perish."*

On the other hand, it is Jesus' faithful followers that truly live the abundant life. They are the ones that are truly blessed and are truly prosperous, because they are right with God and are blessed with much joy and happiness. Even through their times of tribulation they are overjoyed by

Christ because they are filled with His love and therefore, are able to get through the most difficult times. Most importantly they have received the greatest blessing and joy of them all — the eternal crown of life.

How can we decipher between the Real Truth of God and the deceptions of Satan?

Where there is no truth, there are lies and Satan is the father of all lies and the master of deceptions! Satan is very subtle and the Bible says that he blinds the minds of the unbelievers and he also blinds the minds of the believers that have not studied and do not have faith in the Word of God. Without faith in Jesus Christ, <u>WE WILL ALL MOST CERTAINLY FALL</u> into the lies and the deceptions of Satan. Lack of faith opens us up to satanic deception. Satan can most definitely twist the truth of God and make it sound good to those who lack faith. We are so used to being lied to by Satan and man that when we finally do hear the Real Truth (God's Word), we still believe the lies. For example, we were taught in school that man has come from evolution and we have trusted mankind by teaching us this way. Therefore, because of trusting man, many of us have not researched or even thought about the possibility of creation by a supreme being — God. Let me explain further.

Another example would be that many people believe it is acceptable to celebrate Halloween, but when we observe

Halloween we are actually celebrating sin, death, and demons. I encourage you to research the history of Halloween. It is a powerfully influenced deception and without doubt possesses the influential traits of Satanism. This point is proven by the many demonic and sinful costumes that we wear and by the demonic decorations we have scattered all over our front lawns and more so than we do Christmas decorations, not to mention that many of our Christmas ornaments have nothing to do with the true meaning of Christmas anyhow, which brings me to my next point.

When we celebrate Christmas we are missing the whole point of why we celebrate it. The true Gift of Christmas has been exchanged and discarded for another one of Satan's twisted influential deceptions. Satan will do anything to keep our minds away from the true meaning of Christmas and anything else that has to do with God. It is not about pushing and shoving people and knocking them over to get what we need. It is not about stressing ourselves to the point where we cannot wait until Christmas is over. It is not about the gifts that we give each other. It is not about standing outside on line in the early hours of the morning, waiting for the retail store to open so we can buy an exclusive item that they are promoting, before they sell out. It is not about buying expensive gifts and whose gift is more exclusive. We stress ourselves by trying to out-give and in the process, we get over-charged, we over-spend and we put ourselves in debt. We have a false understanding of why we exchange gifts and have blown the whole tradition out of proportion and because of it, we have changed the true meaning of Christmas. Our tradition of gift exchange began with the gifts the Magi brought to Jesus after His birth. They were excited when they found out that their King was born and celebrated His birth by visiting Him, worshiping Him, and giving Him gifts. But this has all changed. Christmas has been made out to be an overly commercialized secular business and the celebration of Christ's birth has been turned into a celebration of mammon! (Evil influence of material wealth and greed).

Christmas is not even about St Nick, although he was a good man, He and other saints are not our Savior. St. Nick did not sacrifice Himself on the cross for mankind as Jesus did. So it is absolutely not about Santa Claus and his reindeers. We give gifts, we feast, and we also adore Santa Claus, whom is not even real, and the One thing that is real and important, and is to be remembered before anything else, is forgotten in all of this. Christmas is about the gift that God has given to the world in the form of His Son Jesus Christ! The true meaning of Christmas is about rejoicing in the birth of our Lord and Savior Jesus Christ! We need to know the true meaning of why Christmas is celebrated and we need to teach our children as well. So when they have children they will be able to teach them the correct way. Christmas is the best time to teach our children about Jesus Christ and the younger they are the better it is because it is easier to get through to them at a younger age. But instead, we rather envelop them with many gifts and spoil them and use this time to teach them about Santa Claus and other false nonsense about Christmas. We believe that we are doing good by giving them many gifts and teaching them the false way in celebrating traditions. But the truth is, if you truly care for your child's wellbeing, safety, and their eternity, then you need to be a better example for them and teach them the right way — that Jesus Christ is our true giver of gifts and that He has given us the best and greatest gift possible. He has given us His crucifixion in order to grant us eternal life. On Christmas read your children the story of His birth and present to them the greatest gift and the greatest miracle that God has given to us — Jesus Christ. By teaching them at a young age you will give them a chance to accept Christ early in their life and they will grow up to be righteous and not prone to be spoiled, self-absorbed, and rebellious, thus being an inspiration and a breath of fresh air to society. If you are able to introduce Santa Claus to your children, then why not introduce Jesus Christ to them? He is the One why we have been given this holiday; He is the true hero of Christmas and our true hero above all. Santa Claus cannot save us, only Jesus Christ can. Santa Claus should have nothing to do with Christmas and he should not be a Christmas icon as we have made him out to be. Besides do you really want to teach your children about someone that has the word Satan in the midst of his name — Santa-Satan? Take the n that is in the middle of the word Santa and put it at the end of the word. What do you get? You get Satan! Remember that Satan can also come as an angel of light. So replace Santa Claus for Jesus Christ and make Christ your Christmas and daily icon. Once we understand the true meaning of Christmas and celebrate it for what it should be, we will then most certainly see all of its glory. If you are a true believer and a faithful follower of Christ, then it is up to you to remind the world what Christmas is all about. Remember that we are God's witnesses and we are to be salt and light.

Easter is another example of Satan twisting the true meaning of Jesus' day and trying to keep our minds far away from Him as possible. Many of us instead of celebrating the death and resurrection of Jesus Christ and recognize the free gift that He has given us, for anyone that accepts it, we rather stray away from the true meaning and believe the things that have absolutely nothing to do with celebrating Easter. For example, Easter bunnies, baskets of candy, jellybeans, and coloring eggs should have nothing to do with Easter. We should be using our time wisely and on this day especially to learn about Jesus Christ and what it means to truly recognize what He has done for us on the cross. Once again, many of us fail to realize ourselves what is most important and it greatly affects our children and it goes as far as affecting us as a nation as well. We continually reject God in order to satisfy our own ways. Mark 7:9 says: *He said to them, "All too well you reject the commandment of God, that you may keep your tradition."*

I would also like to mention that many of us were taught at a young age and were brought up with the idea that the sacraments — baptism, the cup of communion that we receive will forgive us and save us eternally, rather than relying on the fact that it is faith in Jesus Christ that will save us from our sins. We believe that each step of the sacraments that we receive will get us closer to heaven. Faith precedes the sacraments. It is explained in detail in the question labeled — Is baptism a requirement for salvation? And so, let us not buy into Satan's influences because they will keep us away from the Real Truth. If we do not wake up and if we continue to pursue and practice Satan's ways, we will continually be led down the wrong path, which will lead to a life of misery and eventually an unfortunate end.

Sadly we were raised with all these beliefs and many others and over time they have become a part of the fixture. Therefore, we have never questioned them. We have been powerfully influenced by these ideas, false doctrines and false traditions and they have been embedded in us for so long that it has become the way of life and truth for us. We have become ignorant of the Real Truth because of our many years in trusting and believing the lies, and it is almost impossible to change our ways when we have believed in one way for so long. Our ignorance has us believing the lies and our pride has us believing we are right in our ways that when the many times that God sends us the Real Truth (God's Word), we reject it, hence we still believe the lies. Jesus says in Luke 11:35: *"Therefore take heed that the light which is in you is not darkness."* We have believed man and have trusted him to find all the answers for us and the fact is, we have been exposed to so many lies that our beliefs that have come from trusting in mankind and ourselves may not be leading us in the right direction and they will most certainly not save us. We have been following man and have let him dictate our beliefs and our way of life. We cannot trust man because mankind is not perfect and their imperfections — greed, pride, self-centeredness, self-righteousness, and irresponsibility will lead us all to lies! Therefore, we must turn to Jesus Christ and follow Him and trust only in Him for all the answers if we desire to live a life of truth, peace and happiness, and to be eternally saved.

We need to wake up and realize that Satan not only comes as darkness but as I have stated earlier, he can also disguise himself as an angel of light and can deceive us in many ways through mankind. In order to decipher between the Real Truth of God and deceptions of Satan, you must seek out and accept Jesus Christ, repent of your sins, practice constant prayer, have complete faith and by testing all things with God's Word (the Bible). Once you truly commit yourself to Christ you will feel a peace within you, an indescribable calmness that can only be felt from the Spirit of

God. That peace you feel within you is God's way of guiding you and filling you with the Real Truth. You will know the difference between the truth and deception because everything will stand out and will feel right to you when the Spirit of God has led you. When we study the Bible and believe God's promise He will give us faith and it will open our eyes to the divine truth.

We need to make real use of the time that we have left on earth and seek out the Real Truth, while we still have the chance! If we choose to believe the deceptions of Satan and not be willing to search out the truth for ourselves, we can be assured to live a life of lies and misery and not only that, but we will also open the door for Satan to bring us to our eternal doom. Once we have sought out the truth and have accepted it, then we must practice and obey it as well in order to grow in Christ. John 8:31 says: *Then Jesus said to those Jews who believed Him, "If you abide in My word, you are My disciples indeed.* Be aware of Satan's many deceptions because he will do anything to take your life and soul away from you and from the Arms of God. Stop living the lie and turn to Jesus with faith for your source of wisdom and discernment and let God's Word (the Bible) guide you. Your life and soul depend on it!

I'm very confused with the different teachings of each minister or spiritual leader. Who is truly teaching according to God's Word?

Many ministers are <u>DEFINITELY NOT</u> teaching according to God's Word and people are suffering for it. 1 Timothy 1:7 says: *"...desiring to be teachers of the law, understanding neither what they say nor the things which they affirm."* Sadly, many people have become confused and it has become extremely difficult to make a genuine decision for Christ. Many ministers of whom we put our faith in to teach us the right way are not passing on the gospel that saves. With all the conflicting messages that are out there, people are confused with the gospel that saves. To be saved and assured of eternal life our faith must rest solely and entirely in Jesus Christ and what He has accomplished for mankind through His death, His burial and His resurrection. The real trouble is that the pure Word of God has been overcast with so much human ballast, burdensome rules and regulations, and false hopes and consolations. The true Word of God has been filled with much politics and legalism and many spiritual leaders declare we need to follow their rules or else we are not considered believers. It is coupled with human ego demands that others do exactly what they are supposed to do, even if those religious people themselves cannot do what their own rules and regulations say. They become legalistic and they look down on those who cannot meet their standards and expectations. The word "legalism" is not found in the Bible but it is a term used to describe a doctrinal position that puts emphasis on a self-imposed set of rules and regulations and legalists believe in and demand a strict obedience to them. Doctrinally, it is opposed to the grace of God. When spiritual leaders preach they must not do it by their own ability and rules, they must let the Holy Spirit lead them in their teaching so it glorifies God through Jesus Christ and as a result, people will feel a true sense of security. 1 Peter 4:11 says: *"If anyone speaks, let him speak as the oracles of God. If anyone ministers, let him do it as with the ability which God supplies, that in all things God may be glorified through Jesus Christ, to whom belong the glory and the dominion forever and ever."* Amen. The Holy Spirit has a particular mission for the church, and it is only when it is followed that the church will grow the way God intends. Spiritual leaders need to help people understand their part in the world so they can deploy their gifts to participate in God's mission. The purpose of the congregation is to engage the world in bringing God's redemptive work in Christ to all walks of life. Those who hold a legalistic position often fail to see the real purpose for God's Will and His law. Galatians 3:24 says: *"Therefore the law was our tutor to bring us to Christ, that we might be justified by faith."* Legalists may appear to be righteous and spiritual, but legalism ultimately fails to accomplish God's purposes, because legalism is an outward performance rather than an inward spiritual change. Legalists talk about purity while hiding lives riddled with sin and that is why there is no spiritual change within them. Legalism is not an optional path to spirituality. Man-made rules and rituals give people a false sense of security because it does not have the right substances and the peace that people are longing for. The choice between Christ's teaching on spirituality and the false teachers' views is a choice between hiding our sin and victory over our sin! God is not interested in the religion we invent; He simply wants us to obey Him. Do not subject yourself to any religion of human regulations. Instead, trust in Christ to cleanse you from all sin by His blood, and to lead you in the way of righteousness. Understand that legalism does not restrain the flesh and therefore, there is absolutely no spiritual value and no value for salvation found in the legalistic commands of a self-imposed religion. No human work can be added to the merit of Christ's death. His work on the cross is the only acceptable work in God's eyes. Legalists tell us what we can and cannot do but it is all a matter of their own doctrine and not God's law. Colossians 2:20-23 says: *Therefore, if you died with Christ from the basic principles of the world, why, as though living in the world, do you subject yourselves to regulations— "Do not touch, do not taste, do not handle," which all concern things which perish with the using—according to the commandments and doctrines of men? These things indeed have an appearance of wisdom in self-imposed religion, false humility, and neglect of the body, but are of no value against the indulgence of the flesh.* Legalists feel so strongly about their rules and non-essential doctrines that they will chase others out of their fellowship, not even allowing the expression of another viewpoint. These ignorant ways are not the ways of God, these are things that man has added and unfortunately legalism and all of its nonsense has driven many away from our Lord and Savior Jesus Christ.

The true Word of God is actually meant to be a liberating gospel of grace. We are not to be instructed but rather to be gracious to one another. Many spiritual teachers have left out the teaching of God's gospel of grace and have people believing God is a controlling God, rather than a loving and forgiving God. Therefore, many believers that trust this way of teaching have grown stressed in trying to follow Him. Sadly, they feel a legal love because of this type of teaching and they are missing out on what God really is — gracious love. Their faith does not bring them joy as it should. Instead, they feel it is mostly about obligation, duty, and responsibility. Many believers go through their whole life looking for acceptance from God, when they have already been accepted. They also try to find many different ways to please Him, but He already loves them unconditionally. It is not about doing things to become right with God and trying to please Him with our own pompous works and activities. It is about the believer centering their life around Christ — living by faith and love, and letting Christ live through his or her life. They need to let go of their self-righteous ways and trust Jesus with every aspect of their life and follow His ways. Then he or she will live in a real and exciting union with Christ and will experience His full forgiveness, complete acceptance, and unconditional love. This will motivate spiritual maturity, leading to emotional stability. A believer who does not center their life around Christ and does not live by faith, and without any knowledge of the new covenant scriptures, will live from the old patterns of the flesh — the carnal state of mind — fleshly desires — their ways rather than Christ's' ways and will experience emotional instability, and they will be a vehicle of conflict rather than of love, peace, and harmony. Romans 8:6-7 says: *"For to be carnally minded is death, but to be spiritually minded is life and peace. Because the carnal mind is enmity against God."*

The problem with the traditional church is that they do not give people the resources they need to understand faith and understand God's grace — His unconditional love and forgiveness. Most believers today are not aware of what the New Testament teaches because they have not studied it carefully, and they rely on the teachings of their so called spiritual leaders. If your faith is not bringing you joy and you are feeling that you are not growing spiritually in your church, then it may be time for you to move on. Church is necessary because the fellowship in the church is very important. The church will encourage you in your times of difficulty and it is also important for your growth in Christ. At the same time you may be a light, an inspiration, and an encouragement for others in that church and you will just simply enjoy each others fellowship, whether it is for support or just enjoyment. But you need to find the one that teaches the truth or you will never be happy or grow spiritually, and you will always feel a false sense of security. The right church will bring you joy and it will help you replace the wrong thoughts that you may have about God, with thoughts that line up with the Bible's truth, and you will therefore grow spiritually in Christ's love. Understand that when your joy level is down you become much more vulnerable to temptation. So free yourself of all the anxieties in your walk with Christ because God did not intend for it to be a duty and obligation. Man's pride, irresponsibility, and their hunger of desiring power and control have caused many hardships and confusion in the church and in our walk with Christ. This incorrect way of teaching is called organized religion. Religion controls, it segregates, it divides, it enslaves, it is confined by traditions and it is burdensome. That is not the way of God. If you do not understand God's gracious love then you have religion, which are many of man's self-imposed sets of rules that are controlling and manipulating. Rather it is intended to be a beautiful and intimate personal relationship with God the Father and His Son Jesus Christ. Religion is the enemy of God's grace and it is not the way to a true and healthy relationship with Him. God wants us to rest and find peace in Him, <u>NOT</u> feel burdened! Matthew 11:28-29 says: *"Come to Me, all you who labor and are heavy laden, and I will give you rest. Take My yoke upon you and learn from Me, for I am gentle and lowly in heart, and you will find rest for your souls."* In no way is God a dictator and nor does He desire to control us, that is why we have free will. It is man that desires to control us and have authority over us. We are to be filled with all of God's fullness — His love, His wisdom, His joy, His grace, and His peace that is beyond our understanding. In addition, we are to have the kindness and gentleness of Jesus Christ. Ephesians 3:19 says: *"...and to know the love of Christ which passes knowledge; that you may be filled with all the fullness of God.* We are meant to be exactly like Christ and to be filled with all His fullness and God <u>DOES NOT</u> want us to settle for anything less. If we settle for anything less, then we are actually disgracing God. That is the awesome grace of God!

Moving forward, many other spiritual teachers will lecture about the gathering of coins — money. These false teachers twist the truth of the scriptures and do not teach what is important. They will teach that Jesus Christ will bless them with much material wealth if they let go of some of their own money first. They preach if you plant a one thousand dollar seed for their ministry, God will give back one hundred fold, which is true, God will give back a hundred, sixty, thirty fold of what is sown, but that is not the heart and the saving grace of the gospel, it is only a benefit and anyhow, it will only benefit us if it is given for the right reasons and for the right cause. If a seed is unselfishly and sincerely planted toward God's purpose, it will bless us and others in many ways.

While not ignoring the blessings of following Jesus Christ, we must proclaim the need to follow Jesus because He is God, and we owe Him everything. What is right before God, and what glorifies Him, is more important than whatever benefit we may gain. When the gospel is presented for the purpose of material gains, it makes followers of Jesus Christ completely unprepared for tough times and unaware of their need for salvation. After all, if Jesus does not work for us, why not try something else? Also, this approach takes the focus off Jesus Himself, and puts the focus on what He will give us. Many have their hearts set on the blessings, not the One who blesses us. We need to be concerned about what glorifies God and not what benefits self. Do not be deceived by ministers or any spiritual teachers who do not speak the truth — who preach empty words — who give false hope — who preach of false blessings, because you as well will be held accountable if you trust in them. Ephesians 5:6 says: *"Let no one deceive you with empty words, for because of these things the wrath of God comes upon the sons of disobedience."* You need to understand the Bible in order that you do not get misled by these types of false teachers.

These false teachers and their ministries only motive is money and their only true God is gold. Though these so called spiritual leaders use God's name, their true purpose is most certainly all about money, rather than teaching the Word of God and accomplishing His Will. They are nothing but a den of thieves and cause much despair. Matthew 21:13 says *"...And He said to them, "It is written, 'My house shall be called a house of prayer,' but you have made it a 'den of thieves."* They are hypocrites and will receive their just punishment. Proverbs 19:5 says: *"A false witness will not go unpunished, and he who speaks lies will not escape."*

When we give, we need to give for the purpose of God, and not for our own selfish means. We need to contribute our money as well as our time and effort toward God's Will but as I was saying, we must first understand God's Word (the Bible), so we do not get misled. Do not be so desperate and quick to run to these lectures of money like many do, because of wealth they so desperately desire. Do not be fooled and do not give for the wrong reasons. If you are willing to give for your own selfish motives and do not understand God's Word, you will be deceived into making a bad transaction. You will lose your money and waste the time that you should be using in truly knowing God and understanding His Word. God intends for every faithful follower to contribute to His cause and experience blessings and deep spiritual growth as a result, but we must be aware of whom we are contributing to because it will only be our own fault if we contribute to false doctrine. When you feel you have been led to the right cause by the Holy Spirit, then do not hold back. Give with all your heart and with good intentions to help the purpose of God — to spread the good news of the gospel. Do it because you want to help the cause and have faith that God will help you and give back to you in return. God desires to bless all of His believers spiritually and physically but you must first be willing to hear the gospel, understand it, and obey it, you need to walk by faith, you must seek out God's Will, and you must also be willing to let go of all your selfish and fleshly desires. Matthew 13:23 says: *"But he who received seed on the good ground is he who hears the word and understands* it, who indeed bears fruit and produces: some a hundred-fold, some sixty, some thirty."

Another problem with many spiritual leaders is that barely any of them these days would even dare to preach about Satan and hell. They only preach what people want to hear and most people do not want to hear about hell because they feel threatened and scared. Some ministers go with the flow so they do not lose anyone in their church but it is only for their own gain. They should be teaching God's law in its entirety and not add or takeaway from it. Revelation 22:18-19 says: *"For I testify to everyone who hears the words of the prophecy of this book: If anyone adds to these things, God will add to him the plagues that are written in this book; and if anyone takes away from the words of the book of this prophecy, God shall take away his part from the Book of Life, from the holy city, and from the things which are written in this book."* They are too busy building their personal kingdoms and their financial empire is more important to these leaders. If they teach the proper way and are concerned for the people rather than themselves, in turn God will bless them in another way. They should not be focused on losing parishioners and therefore, losing money that is attached to that cause. Jesus spoke of hell more then heaven and more than any other subject in the Bible. It is very vital that people know the reality of Satan and hell and know that he is the mastermind behind all the lies and deceptions. It <u>MOST DEFINITELY</u> needs to be brought into the light whether people like it or not. When something is hard to comprehend, especially when it comes to Satan and demons we usually do not believe in it. In any case, that is irrelevant because Satan does exist and he is alive and well. It is reality to the core! It must <u>ALWAYS</u> be preached for the good of the people so they can be aware of his existence and be aware of his capability of blinding mankind from their sins, to the point of eternal destruction!

We are warned that Satan uses professing men of God — the ministers of righteousness to deceive the church. Satan uses counterfeit ministers whom appear authentic but they are far from being genuine. 2 Corinthians 11:13-15 says: *"For such are false apostles, deceitful workers, transforming themselves into apostles of Christ. And no wonder! For Satan himself transforms himself into an angel of light. Therefore it is no great thing if his ministers also transform themselves into ministers of righteousness, whose end will be according to their works."* The Bible calls Satan "the god of this world," but only until Jesus comes back to reclaim

His land and His true followers. Jesus told the hypocritical spiritual leaders of His day that their father is the devil. John 8:44 says: *"You are of your father the devil, and the desires of your father you want to do. He was a murderer from the beginning, and does not stand in the truth, because there is no truth in him. When he speaks a lie, he speaks from his own resources, for he is a liar and the father of it."*

A number of spiritual leaders are immoral; they are wolves in sheep's clothing and perform immoral acts. God warns them about irresponsibility, greed, and pride. His righteous judgment will first be upon those hypocrites of His law and with a more severe judgment because people look up to them and trust them to teach them the right ways of God. James 3:1 says: *"My brethren, let not many of you become teachers, knowing that we shall receive a stricter judgment."* Do not ever get turned away from Jesus Christ and lose faith because of these immoral principles and teachings of some spiritual leaders. Whoever teaches lies and carries out their own will are not true men of God.

If you are a faithful follower of Christ and you are already armed with some spiritual knowledge and have a true love for God, but are still confused, then you may be still spiritually immature. Your wisdom and knowledge may still be underdeveloped because you may not be exercising your faith as you should be. Let the Word of God (the Bible) and prayer guide you so you will not be deceived. Ask Christ to help you find the right spiritual teachers and you must truly trust in Him that He will lead you to the right ones, because trusting in Christ is what faith is all about. He will show you who your true teachers are and who speak the truth and in turn, they will help you grow in the Lord. Genuine spiritual leaders are humble and also walk humbly before our God. True spiritual leaders do not just teach from the pulpit and then walk away from people, but they like to help them on a personal level as well. They make an effort to make personal contact and minister to them personally.

Many people are appalled by some Christians and it is because of their wrong and brutal way in teaching the truth. The congregation and church leaders alike have done a poor job in teaching and representing the Lord. They infiltrate their own man-made rules and their own very harsh and unloving way of teaching and do not teach by what the scriptures tell us, and as I have mentioned earlier, if we do not abide by their rules then we are not considered believers. Many cannot understand and many do not teach the message of grace, which is we are not saved by the works of man's law, but we are saved by God's grace through the works of faith in Jesus Christ and when taught in this correct way, you can be rest assured that it is taught in a loving way as well, by Christ's faithful followers who have this accurate knowledge and wisdom, and love of the truth. The good news is that, although these people who are appalled by some Christians, find Jesus very appealing because He has expressed truth, love, and grace through His divine life. As I have stated, God does in fact have many righteous and faithful spiritual leaders and congregations at work for Him that do represent Him in the right and loving way. It is in your best interest by faith to let Christ guide you in that way. Ephesians 4:11-14 says: "...*And He Himself gave some to be apostles, some prophets, some evangelists, and some pastors and teachers, for the equipping of the saints for the work of ministry, for the edifying of the body of Christ, till we all come to the unity of the faith and of the knowledge of the Son of God, to a perfect man, to the measure of the stature of the fullness of Christ; that we should no longer be children, tossed to and fro and carried about with every wind of doctrine, by the trickery of men, in the cunning craftiness of deceitful plotting.*" I cannot stress enough to let prayer and the light of God's Word (the Bible), guide you in your walk with Christ and test all religious leaders and all things with the Bible to see if they are true. Isaiah 8:20 says: *"To the law and to the testimony! If they do not speak according to this word, it is because there is no light in them."*

Is baptism a requirement for salvation?

If our trust and confidence for eternity is in baptism, rather than faith in Christ, then what hope do we have? Anyone teaching that you have to be dunked in water to be saved is not teaching the gospel. You have to be saved first, otherwise you are just coming up a wet sinner. Baptism is for those who are already saved. It is an outward show and a sign of one's faith. Once again, to be saved and assured of eternal life our faith must rest solely and entirely in Jesus Christ and what He has accomplished for mankind through His death, His burial and His resurrection. Do not let water baptism become the focus of our faith; it is Jesus Christ and His death and resurrection that is to be the focus of our faith. Some time ago, I encountered a pastor. He informed me that I needed to be baptized to be saved. I told him that I already have been baptized, and then I asked him, "Am I saved?" He answered "no!" Then he started explaining to me how in order to be saved, I needed to be baptized in his church. To top it off there was no mention of the death, burial and resurrection of Jesus Christ. Although his intentions may have been good in some way and in his understanding of the gospel, he did not once mention to me the all important gospel that saves.

Water baptism is not a requirement to get into heaven. The thief on the cross next to Jesus was never baptized. Is he going to hell? No, because he had faith that Jesus Christ was the true Messiah. It was his faith that saved Him. Luke 23:39-43 says: *Then one of the criminals who were hanged blasphemed Him, saying, "If You are the Christ, save Yourself and us." But the other, answering, rebuked him, saying, "Do you not even fear God, seeing you are under the same condemnation? And we indeed justly, for we receive the due reward of our deeds; but this Man has done nothing wrong." Then he said to Jesus, "Lord, remember me when You come into Your kingdom." And Jesus said to him, "Assuredly, I say to you, today you will be with Me in Paradise."*

The water does not open our eyes to sin and change man's heart. Only Jesus can do that by faith. Baptism is not a work that saves you and nothing can wash away sin but the blood of Jesus Christ. Many people have been baptized as infants, yet they still live a sinful life because water does not change us. They have never asked Christ for forgiveness and have never put their faith in Him, which is the only means of spiritual transformation. Therefore, they still do not have a divine holy nature, which would keep them from sinning. Sadly, countless numbers of people continue to sin because of their unchanged hearts and are trusting in their infancy baptism to be saved. Baptism will not get you into heaven as many people believe. Accepting the free gift of salvation that Christ has given us is the only possible way that the Holy Spirit will work within us to change our hearts from continuous sinning.

Water baptism is an outward sign showing that one has accepted Jesus as their Lord and Savior and that he or she plans to obey Jesus and live to please Him. When a person is saved and understands what baptism means, he or she should be baptized and will want to be baptized. Once you are buried in the water you are raised a new person, not as a result of the water, but as a result of the transforming grace of Christ, which the water points to — faith in Christ. Baptism will not spiritually change you and give you the faith you need to be saved. Faith precedes baptism and not the other way around, then you will begin to feel an inward spiritual change and therefore, you will feel the need to be baptized. If a person does not repent and does not have faith, they will continue to be spiritually dead and therefore, he or she will not feel the need to be baptized. Baptism is for those who have chosen to follow Jesus Christ through faith, and they now know the significance of baptism, and are excited to get baptized in their walk with Him.

Baptism is a symbol and it symbolizes putting to death our fleshly desires, thus living of the spirit and following Christ, which many whom were baptized as infants do not do or even realize. It is proven in what I have just stated, that baptism does not inwardly change us spiritually, and as a result, in being spiritually dead, it does not open our eyes to sin. If we have not realized the true meaning of our infancy baptism then we have not put our fleshly desires behind us, and we are not following the way of Christ. Therefore, we are still spiritually dead and as a result, we are still living in sin — living for our own worldly desires — living our way, rather than living of the spirit and trusting and following Jesus Christ. Once again, baptism <u>DOES NOT</u> change our hearts or cleanse us from our sins. It is only by faith through Christ that our sins are washed away and we are made spiritually alive and given a holy nature, not by any water! Only then will our eyes be opened and we will inherit the blessings of the Holy Spirit that keep our hearts away from sin, thus being eternally saved. Galatians 5:22-23 says: *"But the fruit of the Spirit is love, joy, peace, longsuffering, kindness, goodness, faithfulness, gentleness, self-control."* For the fruits of the Holy Spirit is the character of God Himself.

You are probably asking me by now, then why were many of us baptized as infants? Baptizing infants is nowhere to be found in God's Word because you do have to be aware of why you are being baptized, and babies are not yet aware of the gospel, so they cannot accept it or reject it. Infancy baptism is only to encourage parents to pray for their child and to train their child properly in the Word of God, with the purpose and hope that he or she may believe and have faith, and accept Christ when they are old enough to understand.

I would also like to mention another one of Satan's strong delusions that he sends upon us that people trust in to be saved. It is another symbol and many receive it unworthily because they do not understand the meaning behind it — communion. People are receiving it and yet their sins are not yet forgiven by Christ because they have not sought out the true message of salvation, and have not understood the truth and therefore, have not repented of their sins. The church is filled with unconverted people who have never seen and have never been taught that their sinful cravings are unclean. We have multitudes in pews that see sin as acceptable, so they look at God as their servant. Instead of saying, "God let me serve you," they say "I want more!" They are receiving the cup of communion for all the wrong reasons. We cannot disobey Christ time and time again and then believe by receiving communion each time, that everything is fine again and we are forgiven. Absolutely not! Many believe in communion to save them as well as baptism and as a result, they ignore the truth. They continually go about their own way and still constantly sin after receiving communion, for the reason that they do not see that their sins are unclean, because communion as well as baptism does not spiritually change us. It does not open our eyes and our hearts to the deceitfulness of sin and therefore, we believe that our sins are harmless, and as a result we continue on sinning. Only faith in Christ can open our eyes to our sinful deeds and change our hearts. Satan wants us to believe by receiving communion, it is good enough to be forgiven and by routinely receiving it week after week and with no idea of the truth, because we have not sought it out for ourselves; sadly we do believe that it does suffice and we are forgiven by God. We are not children of God if we have not had a spiritual rebirth, have not come to faith, and have not sincerely confessed our sins to Jesus Christ.

If you have read your Bible and you must, then you will know that the church ordinances — a church ritual that is thought to have saving values, are visual aids to help us better understand and appreciate what Jesus Christ has accomplished for us in His redemptive work and that they do not have any saving values whatsoever. Each step of the sacraments that many of us receive and have received does not get us closer to heaven, as many of us believe. Only Jesus Christ can save. The cup of communion and baptism are not acts that will save us because they are both an outward performance, instead of an inward change. Are you trusting and have been trusting in an outward visible sign without experiencing an inward spiritual change?! Have faith and trust in Christ and do not rely on the sacraments to save you! One of the reasons for the ineffectiveness of the church today is because of the confusion that surrounds this matter. Baptism and communion are only secondary and we need to focus on the primary, which is God's message of salvation. That is the only gospel that saves. Once again only faith in Christ will the Holy Spirit work in us to renew our minds and change us on the inside, therefore opening our eyes to the filth of sin, thus turning us away from our sinful actions, and resulting in our eternal salvation.

Once you have truly accepted Christ and have repented of your sins, then water baptism and communion as well will have significance. You will understand the importance and true meaning of both and you will want to get baptized and receive communion in your walk with Christ. Your response of heart in repentance and in faith will then be symbolized and identified in the fact of your baptism and receiving communion. Receive Gods' Word first with faith and then be baptized. Acts 2:38, 41 says: *Then Peter said to them, "Repent, and let every one of you be baptized in the name of Jesus Christ for the remission of sins; and you shall receive the gift of the Holy Spirit. Then those who gladly received his word were baptized; and that day about three thousand souls were added to them.*

Salvation is not brought about by any of man's religious creeds, systems, ceremonies, joining a church, baptism and communion. No man or organization can do anything to you that will make you a child of God. Join what you will, go through ceremony after ceremony, memorize creeds, and try to keep the rules and regulations of man-made systems and principles, but it will not save you! Only by a spiritual rebirth by faith through Christ will!

If I am a good person can I receive eternal salvation by the good that I have done in my life? Will that compensate for the bad or actually the not so bad that I have done in my life?

This is one of the biggest misconceptions that the world is facing and it is one of the most powerful of deceptions. Titus 3:5-7 says: *"...not by works of righteousness which we have done, but according to His mercy He saved us, through the washing of regeneration and renewing of the Holy Spirit, whom He poured out on us abundantly through Jesus Christ our Savior, that having been justified by His grace we should become heirs according to the hope of eternal life."* No matter how good you are or what good you do or have done, unless you have been made a partaker of the divine nature by a spiritual rebirth through faith in Jesus Christ you are not saved. When you were born the first time, you were made a partaker of the old nature, the sinful nature we all received from Adam. The nature of Adam is fallen, corrupt, and completely depraved and we as humans have the same nature so we need to be cleansed of our sins. When you are born again — the spiritual rebirth, you become a partaker of the divine nature and are also then forgiven of your sins. We cannot truly be good because of our fleshly sinful nature and because of our fleshly desires. Therefore, we cannot be forgiven and gain salvation, and be children of God if we desire the worldly pleasures rather than the pleasures of the spirit.

God tells us that our good is like filthy rags. Isaiah 64:6 says: *"But we are all like an unclean thing, And all our righteousnesses are like filthy rags; We all fade as a leaf, And our iniquities, like the wind, Have taken us away."* So we need a new nature — a divine holy nature to truly be righteous and God transforms us and gives us that the new nature and forgives us of our sins the moment we receive His Son Jesus Christ. We will then be Christ-like and be children of God and will have gained everlasting life. We will be living and enjoying the spirit filled life and no longer of the flesh that causes us to live in sin, which leads to hopelessness, and misery and eventually eternal separation from God. Our trouble is not on the outside, but we need an interior transformation. In the scriptures it is stated that God spoke these words of a new birth to Nicodemus — a good man who did His best to gain heaven and still could not enter it until He was given a spiritual nature. *John 3:1-6 says: There was a man of the Pharisees named Nicodemus, a ruler of the Jews. This man came to Jesus by night and said to Him, "Rabbi, we know that You are a teacher come from God; for no one can do these signs that You do unless God is with him." Jesus answered and said to him, "Most assuredly, I say to you, unless one is born again, he cannot see the kingdom of God." Nicodemus said to Him, "How can a man be born when he is old? Can he enter a second time into his mother's womb and be born?" Jesus answered, "Most assuredly, I say to you, unless one is born of water and the Spirit, he cannot enter the kingdom of God. That which is born of the flesh is flesh, and that which is born of the Spirit is spirit.* So if Nicodemus could not have gained heaven although a good man, then what makes us think that we can? Heaven is a Holy place and no one person can enter it until God has given us a holy nature and has forgiven us of our sins.

The good will never compensate for the bad. Even if you have truly done good in your life, who is going to wipe away the bad or not so bad that you have done and that you are going to do? Luke 13:5 says: *"...I tell you, no; but unless you repent you will all likewise perish."* Only Jesus Christ through His blood has wiped away our past, present and future sins by His death and resurrection and has made us truly righteous, and if you are willing to sincerely accept Christ in your life, then by God's grace He will be willing to forgive all of your sins. If you can receive eternal salvation just by the good compensating for the bad or by just doing some good works, then why did Jesus Christ have to die for our sins? If we can save ourselves and make it on our own then we do not need Jesus. Proverbs 14:12 says: *"There is a way that seems right to a man, but its end is the way of death."* If you are a good person and do some good deeds but you have not placed your faith in Christ as your Lord and Savior, you will not gain eternal salvation. We are not saved by doing good works. 1 John 5:12 says: *"He who has the Son has life; he who does not have the Son of God does not have life."* Good works can truly be good only when they are accomplished in the power of the Holy Spirit given to those who place their faith in Christ. Because of our sinful nature we will never truly be good outside of Christ; we can only be made good by the grace of God through faith in Christ. Every sin no matter what it may be will be forgiven by the grace of God, but one sin that God cannot and will not forgive is rejecting and resisting His Spirit as He is revealing His Son Jesus Christ, because we do need to know that Christ is the only one that has suffered greatly for us in order to give us eternal life through His death and resurrection. We must understand that His selfless act has saved us from the wrath of God. Matthew 12:31 says: *"Therefore I say to you, every sin and blasphemy will be forgiven men, but the blasphemy against the Spirit will not be forgiven men."* It is by God's grace that He sent His only Son Jesus Christ to die for us, and it was the only way possible and still holds today, for mankind's redemption, thus giving us eternal salvation.

When we do not have Christ in our lives it is impossible to see the things of the spirit and we will continue on falsely believing that our sins are not so bad. No matter what bad you do or not so bad, sin is sin and every sin we commit is not right in the eyes of God. Some sins are worse than others and you may think that your sins are not so bad because you have not taken another's life or you have not committed adultery, but we must open our eyes and be aware of sins deceit, and the only way by seeing even the lesser of all sins real danger is to accept Jesus Christ as our Lord and Savior and the Spirit of God will open our eyes. Many do not realize that it is the smaller of sins that blinds us and keeps us separated from God. We take every sin way to lightly and many even believe that lying is no big deal, but it is a huge sin in the eyes of God because by continually lying, it will most certainly harm us in someway. Not only that, but it will without doubt affect others that are exposed to that lie as well. Our sins have a direct or an indirect consequence on others. If you continue on believing in even the least significant of all sins as not being a problem, then you will eventually get deceit as a reward — meaning through the deceitfulness of sin your heart will become hardened and therefore, you will not feel the need to ever have Christ in your life. Unfortunately, this deceptive and misleading idea that many have will keep them from gaining eternal salvation. Hebrews 3:12-13 says: *Beware, brethren, lest there be in any of you an evil heart of unbelief in departing from the living God; but exhort one another daily, while it is called "Today," lest any of you be hardened through the deceitfulness of sin.* Without genuinely having Christ in our lives we do not have the Holy Spirit opening our spiritual eyes to show us how bad sin really is. Without the Holy Spirit opening our spiritual eyes, we have no way of being convicted of our sin and being turned away from it. We need to recognize and accept the fact that we are all sinners. We also need to have faith, and accept the fact that Jesus Christ is truly our Lord and Savior, and that He died on the cross for all of mankind to save us from our sins and that through Him

God has given us eternal salvation. The Holy Spirit will then open our spiritual eyes and the light will expose the darkness of sin. We will be able to see sin for what it really is!

We compare ourselves to others and therefore, we feel that we are not so bad after all. But God does not see it that way. He compares us to Jesus Christ. Jesus has lived a sinless life and He has died for us and then rose again. Next to Him, we cannot help but fall completely short. We do not earn our salvation by good works but once again we are saved according to God's grace through faith in Jesus Christ. Ephesians 2:8-9 says: *"For it is by grace you have been saved, through faith — and this not from yourselves, it is the gift of God — not by works, so that no one can boast."*

God has done everything for mankind and owes us nothing! We owe Him everything! No matter how good we think we are, we have all sinned and no man is righteous in the eyes of God. Romans 3:11-12 says: *"There is none who understands; There is none who seeks after God. They have all turned aside; They have together become unprofitable; There is none who does good, no, not one."* Without faith and repentance of our sins through Jesus Christ, it is impossible to please God. Hebrews 11:6 says: *"But without faith it is impossible to please Him, for he who comes to God must believe that He is, and that He is a rewarder of those who diligently seek Him."*

Many people believe that somehow and in someway they will get to heaven. Others believe that they have earned their way to eternal life by some good works that they do. Many do some good works but they do it for their own selfish reasons anyhow—our fleshly sinful nature. Much of the good works that are done are always done to benefit oneself in one way or another. People are always looking to get something out of it for themselves. When one becomes Christ-like and of the spirit they will no longer have any selfish desires because their new heart and mind will now be focused on serving others to glorify God. As I have stated earlier, good works can truly be good only when they are accomplished in the power of the Holy Spirit given to those who place their faith in Christ. People that believe in these misleading ways of gaining eternal life do not put any thought in or worry about their eternity because they have already put their trust in their ignorance. Mankind has always had a tendency to proclaim themselves innocent and believe that they have never done anything that could possibly prevent them from going to heaven. They also believe that their works will pay for their sins, but their works will not pay for any of their sins, no matter what they do. These people are all self-righteous. A person who is self-righteous is one who believes that they are right with God, based on how well they think and act in life, as opposed to God making them righteous, based on His grace and mercy. Grace meaning we receive something from God that we did not earn (righteousness and eternal life) and do not deserve (eternal life) and mercy meaning that God withholds something we have earned and deserve (punishment). As pleasant and good as one may believe they are, which according to Romans 3:12: *"There is none that does good, no, not one,"* their beliefs would then be putting them in direct contradiction with God. If you think you are good enough to go to heaven and believe that you do not need to put your faith in Jesus Christ for salvation, then you are making God out to be a liar and therefore, you are being self-righteous and prideful, which that alone makes you a sinner. Luke 18:10-14 says: *"Two men went up to the temple to pray, one a Pharisee and the other a tax collector. The Pharisee stood and prayed thus with himself, 'God, I thank You that I am not like other men—extortioners, unjust, adulterers, or even as this tax collector. I fast twice a week; I give tithes of all that I possess.' And the tax collector, standing afar off, would not so much as raise his eyes to heaven, but beat his breast, saying, 'God, be merciful to me a sinner!' I tell you, this man went down to his house justified rather than the other; for everyone who exalts himself will be humbled, and he who humbles himself will be exalted."* Lean not on your own understanding but trust only in Christ. You do not earn eternal salvation by some good works and you do not by somehow and in someway just happen to acquire it, it is a gift! Eternal life is a free gift from God given to you by His good grace when you genuinely repent of your sins through Jesus Christ. Once you have sincerely accepted the message of salvation you will want to do good works anyhow, because with the love of the Holy Spirit being poured out upon you, you will then truly start feeling the love for others. True good works are a result of obedience to and love of Jesus Christ.

These beliefs of many are all of Satan's deceptive devices hard at work. Please take to heart the Real Truth of God and do not be deceived by Satan. You do not want to leave your eternity to guesswork. If you believe that if you are good in general and do some good works, and by that you will end up in heaven, are you confident about your decision? If you are, what do you base your certainty on? If you were to die today are you one hundred percent sure that you will go to heaven? We are not perfect and therefore, that is why God sent us a Savior. He made us perfect and sinless through Jesus Christ so we can receive salvation and enter His Holy Paradise. Only through Jesus we can find our way out of eternal hell and into eternal salvation. John 14:6 says: *"Jesus said to him, 'I am the way, the truth, and the life. No one comes to the Father except through Me.'"* Romans 10:9 says: *"...that if you confess with your mouth the Lord Jesus and believe in your heart that God has raised Him from the dead, you will be saved."*

How important is the Bible? Is it truly the Word of God and will we prosper from it?

Hebrews 4:12 says: *"For the word of God is living and powerful, and sharper than any two-edged sword, piercing even to the division of soul and spirit, and of joints and marrow, and is a discerner of the thoughts and intents of the heart."* The Bible is thus far the best-seller and has been since the beginning of time and rightly so, because the Bible is the most important book that has been ever read and is ever going to be read. When God being the Author, I would not expect anything less than the best. The Bible is God's law book to the human race and He uses the Scriptures to actively and powerfully accomplish His purpose in you and through you to impact the world. The Bible is so important because in it, God reveals Himself and His Will to us and it is the best place to find the answers to hundreds of spiritual questions. The truth is being drowned out by all of the lies and deceptions that are flooding this world and the Bible is the only book that cuts through it all. You need to know your Bible so you can discern when someone is misleading you. The Bible encourages the believer and nonbeliever to be wise and use their minds when investigating the truth.

Often those who question the reliability or usefulness of the Bible have not investigated the matter for themselves. They merely repeat what others say. You cannot prove the Bible wrong if you do your homework. Acts 17:11 says: *"These were more fair-minded than those in Thessalonica, in that they received the word with all readiness, and searched the Scriptures daily to find out whether these things were so."* Instead of being deceived and blindly accepting what others say, we should research it for ourselves because if we do not, we will be held accountable. Proverbs 14:15 says: *"The simple believes every word, but the prudent considers well his steps."* We need to open our hearts to the Word of God (the Bible), in order for our faith to have any chance. Romans 10:17 says: *"So then faith comes by hearing, and hearing by the word of God."* For those who have faith in the Word of God it is simple to understand that it truly is His Word. DO NOT be deceived into believing that the Bible is just another book, because it is not. It truly is God's genuine Word. Because of the influence of Satan, many have tried to destroy the Bible by making it out to be fiction, they have twisted the truth and they have tried to mask it as well. Also many people say that the Bible contradicts itself, but that is not the case. The truth is that we need to understand the

Bible and we must recognize that when Jesus became the Lamb of God by sacrificing Himself on the cross, things changed and we were given grace. We no longer live under the law of the old covenant because Jesus' shed blood that was required for mankind's redemption due to the weakness of our flesh, has fulfilled that law. Romans 8:2-4 says: *"For the law of the Spirit of life in Christ Jesus has made me free from the law of sin and death. For what the law could not do in that it was weak through the flesh, God did by sending His own Son in the likeness of sinful flesh, on account of sin: He condemned sin in the flesh, that the righteous requirement of the law might be fulfilled in us who do not walk according to the flesh but according to the Spirit.* We now live in a new way and live in the age of grace and have been given much more. Hebrews 10:20 says: *"...by a new and living way which He consecrated for us, through the veil, that is, His flesh."* We now live by faith and by grace through Jesus Christ. Jesus became the Mediator of a new and much better covenant after His death and resurrection and He is our example and the Author of our faith today and our means of salvation. Hebrews 5:9 says: *"...And having been perfected, He became the author of eternal salvation to all who obey Him."* We must equip ourselves with the Bibles entirety for wisdom, knowledge and the full understanding of the truth, but our safety, wellbeing, and salvation lies in obeying the New Testament teaching.

The evidence is more than convincing when we honestly consider what the Bible proclaims. The Bible is historically accurate and over the years, skeptics have challenged and continue to challenge the Bible's accuracy regarding the names of people and places it mentions. Time and again, the evidence has proved the skepticism to be unfounded and the Bible record to be trustworthy. The Bible contains hundreds of detailed prophecies relating to the future of individual nations, including Israel, certain cities, and mankind. Other prophecies concern the coming of One who would be the Messiah, the Savior of all who would believe in Him. Unlike the prophecies found in other religious books or those by men such as Nostradamus, biblical prophecies are extremely detailed. There are over three hundred prophecies concerning Jesus Christ in the Old Testament. Not only was it foretold where He would be born and His lineage, but also how He would die and that He would rise again. There simply is no logical way to explain the fulfilled prophecies in the Bible other than by divine origin. There is no other religious book with the extent or type of predictive prophecy that the

Bible contains. Such historical accuracy is what you would expect of a book inspired by God. There are absolute truths in the Bible. Only in the Bible are there accurately fulfilled prophecies of a coming Messiah. Only in the Bible do we have the extremely accurate transmission of the eyewitness documents — scripture, so we can trust what was originally written. There has also been the re-discovery of Noah's ark and in that discovery there is recorded evidence showing that many fish fossils have been found on the tallest of mountains and millions of other remains that had drowned due to the great flood, which was the first of God's worldwide judgments. There has also been the re-discovery of Sodom and Gomorrah and many other archeological finds. These also provide compelling witness and proof to the truthfulness of the Bible.

The practical wisdom contained in the Bible benefits people of all backgrounds. By reading or listening to the Bible, a person is in a place that can be saved by God. Additionally, you will also learn the many awesome and wonderful truths about God. You will learn about His love, His wrath, and His salvation plan. The Bible is so full of wisdom, comfort, direction, and encouragement. Effectively you are hearing the voice of God because God is the Author of the Bible. Revelation 1:3 says: *"Blessed is he who reads and those who hear the words of this prophecy, and keep those things which are written in it; for the time is near."* The Bible tells us that only God can save us and He desires to save us all. God knows those who will come to Him in faith, so He performs the mighty miracle of salvation by applying the Word of God (the Bible), to the hearts and lives of those who are to be saved. The effect of this miracle of salvation on the saved person's life is that now he has a love for God and the Bible. He now is happiest when he is obeying God's Word. Applying biblical principles is beneficial for emotional growth as well. The wisdom found in the Bible can make even an inexperienced person wise. In addition, once we gain confidence in the Bible, it can help us in a way no other book can in taking the next step toward having stronger faith. If you know and understand what the Bible teaches about God, you will avoid being misled and will be able to draw close to Him. Thus, if you are a person who truly desires to become saved, then you should spend much time carefully reading or listening to the Bible. I encourage you all to take the time to saturate yourselves with the Bible, because <u>YOU WILL</u> gain much wisdom in the Word of God and in you the Real Truth will finally be revealed.

We will most definitely prosper from the Bible in many ways if we do what it says. Joshua 1:8 says: *"This Book of the Law shall not depart from your mouth, but you shall meditate in it day and night, that you may observe to do according to all that is written in it. For then you will make your way prosperous, and then you will have good success."* Many are prosperous and successful by earthly and temporal standards, but may not be righteous in the eyes of God. God calls us to be faithful, not successful. But if we are faithful to God's Word, not only will we be righteous in His eyes, which means more than anything, but He can bless us with prosperity and success beyond our comprehension. Even though God can bless us with physical wealth, let us not fail to recognize and forget that it is the spiritual wealth that matters and is unsurpassed, not the physical wealth, and you will see and understand with faith.

We must also be aware that Satan can also give us material wealth, but his wealth comes with a price. He gives us material wealth for his own benefit in order that we use it against God's Will. I have noticed that many people who are not committed to Jesus Christ and have no inclination of God make an ignorant statement and have said that they have been blessed because of their wealth that they have obtained.

In order to be blessed by God you need to be a faithful follower of Jesus Christ and you need to have a desire to seek out and truly know and trust the Word of God. I encourage those to study the Bible to see if it is actually a blessing from God or if it is another one of Satan's deceptions to pull you even further away from God. Rather than a blessing, their wealth may be a curse because the more money and the more possessions people have, the further away their minds are from God. They believe they are invincible because of all the wealth that they have acquired, and by that, they are deceived into believing that they do not need Him and believe they have it all and are self-sufficient. As a result, unfortunately many will never give up their wealth and worldly pleasures in order to follow Christ. Matthew 19:24 says: *"...And again I say to you, it is easier for a camel to go through the eye of a needle than for a rich man to enter the kingdom of God."* Sadly, many wealthy lives have spiraled out of control and have tragically ended, due to the absence of God and His blessings in their life. But Proverbs 10:22 says: *"The blessing of the LORD makes one rich, And He adds no sorrow with it."* Without Christ there is no foundation for our lives. Our foundation needs to be built on Jesus Christ and His wisdom and knowledge, which is made clear in God's Word (the Bible), so that we are anchored securely. Matthew 7:24-27 says: *"Therefore whoever hears these sayings of Mine, and does them, I will liken him to a wise man who built his house on the rock: and the rain descended, the floods came, and the winds blew and beat on that house; and it did not fall, for it was founded on the rock.* *"But everyone who hears these sayings of Mine, and does not do them, will be like a foolish man who built his house on the sand: and the rain descended, the floods came, and the winds blew and beat on that house; and it fell. And great was its fall."* In addition to many lives tragically ending due to their weak foundation because they lacked Christ, many others that are wealthy are far from even being happy and are extremely empty inside, also due to the fact that they are missing the biggest part of their life — Jesus Christ. It does not matter how much money we have and how much material wealth we can obtain, and how prosperous we are by earthly standards, because if we are poor in spirit and lack Christ we have absolutely <u>NOTHING</u>! We will never be truly happy and satisfied and we will ultimately be on our way to our own physical and eternal ruin!

Once again I encourage all to study the Bible because it is the only book that can test the spirits to see if the physical blessings are actually from God. 1 John 4:1 says: *"Beloved, do not believe every spirit, but test the spirits, whether they are of God."* You cannot get a better counselor than the Word of God, (the Bible).

Is self-centeredness a serious and dangerous problem?

Self-centeredness is partnered with pride, arrogance, vanity, and so on, which are all an abomination to God. Self-interest is the most serious and dangerous problem to us and our society and is a major deception that completely dominates our lives. Those of today's generation have taken it to an unprecedented level and seem to take pride in being self-centered. They care for only their needs and wants. They are completely self-driven and are more concerned with their image, their ways, and materialistic things rather than issues that affect the country and the rest of the world. Self-centered people do not even bother to take the time to understand another person's point-of-view or feelings. They are completely inconsiderate to others and do not respect them. They also believe that they are perfect, all knowing, and stand above all. This causes much misery and much harm upon themselves and upon others who are in the way of their futility. Their self-centered morals and ways are ignorant, prideful, useless, and completely meaningless and destructive.

Most importantly, when people are self-absorbed they are entirely oblivious to God and sadly, they do not pay any attention to their spiritual side and their eternity. Psalm 10:4 says: *"The wicked in his proud countenance does not seek God; God is in none of his thoughts."* They are unaware and disobedient to the fact that they will be going before God for judgment at any moment. When we are self-centered we have no care for gaining wisdom and understanding of what really is important in life because the material things, our wants, needs, and our pride mean more to us than anything else and therefore, our physical and eternal state are in danger because of our disobedience to the truth. Very few people even notice their commitment to self-centeredness and among those who do; even fewer are deeply concerned about it. Those who are self-absorbed should be very concerned. Proverbs 10:29 says *"...But destruction will come to the workers of iniquity."*

One must get over oneself and we must humble ourselves before God because it is not about us. Everything flows out of the cesspool of self-centeredness and evil has come upon us as a result of the selfishness of man. Self-centeredness and pride is the enemy of us all and it will be our downfall as it was Satan's, if we continue to let it dominate our lives. Our physical and eternal being depends on God's wisdom and understanding, or both our body and soul will be on their way in paying a tremendous price.

We should become conscious of God and put Him first and foremost in our lives and not trust in ourselves. We need to hand over to Him every aspect of our lives. If you are willing to let go of your self-interest you need to have faith in Jesus Christ and trust in God to remove it for you. Once the Holy Spirit starts a work in you, you will see that your self interest will no longer be important to you. You will be transformed and live a new life, leaving your old ways and habits behind. You will see through the Spirit of God the true meaning of life. Obliterate the self-absorbed life and live the awesome Christ-life. Once we begin the transformation process with the help of God through His Holy Spirit and begin to understand that Christ is our source for all that we are, we will come to see and feel that He is the only way that brings fulfillment, true happiness, peace, and joy. With Christ in your life you will have a real love for others and you will want to honor them above yourself instead of using them for your own selfish desires.

Does God approve
of same-sex marriages?

Same-sex marriages are an abomination to God and therefore, it is not His Will that has turned people to homosexuality. Do not believe the deception that God created people that way. He did not make people that way because He gave mankind free will. Homosexuality is demonic influenced and is considered an immoral act, which is against God's Word. Leviticus 18:22 says: *"You shall not lie with a male as with a woman. It is an abomination."* That is why He has made both man and woman so they can be in companionship with one another as one flesh in marriage. Ephesians 5:30-31 says: *"For we are members of His body, of His flesh and of His bones. For this reason a man shall leave his father and mother and be joined to his wife, and the two shall become one flesh.* No marriage can be sanctioned if the marriage involves acts that put the couple outside of eternal salvation. No matter what our society may legislate, the law of God is clear; a marriage is not a godly marriage if it is a same-sex union. 1 Corinthians 6:9-10 says: *"Do you not know that the unrighteous will not inherit the kingdom of God? Do not be deceived. Neither fornicators, nor idolaters, nor adulterers, nor homosexuals, nor sodomites, nor thieves, nor covetous, nor drunkards, nor revilers, nor extortioners will inherit the kingdom of God.*" If God had intended humankind to be fulfilled through both heterosexual and homosexual marriage, He would have designed our bodies to allow reproduction through both means. Marriage is a sacred and divine institution between man and woman and that needs to be respected.

Many have spread the myth that when it comes to marriage "all you need is love" and that is a big misconception and a great deception. It evidently is not true; it is not a marriage in God's eyes if it is a homosexual one. The law of God's Word cannot be diluted to please these groups. The true Church of God needs to stand strong and not allow the approval of same-sex marriages. God's moral nature is perfectly expressed in a heterosexual unification. Immorality brings crisis to society and God will judge any society that institutes same-sex marriages. If you are willing, then God will be more than happy to delivery you from the bondage of homosexuality that Satan and his fallen angels are subjecting you to.

What does God say about abortions? If He sees it as an offense will He forgive me?

Jeremiah 1:5 says: *"Before I formed you in the womb I knew you; before you were born I sanctified you. I ordained you a prophet to the nations."* God knew this man before he was born. As he was forming in his mother's womb, God gave him his personality, talents, and temperament. If his mother had gotten an abortion, the fetal tissue she aborted would have been a real person named Jeremiah; a mighty prophet of God and the gift of God's voice to the nations. Isaiah 49:1 says: *"The LORD has called Me from the womb; from the matrix of My mother He has made mention of My name."* It is clear that life begins when God creates it, not at some later point in time when it has grown to look like a newborn. God does not judge things according to their stage of development the way humans tend to. Even the tiniest embryo is the subject of His love and care. God sees each of our lives in the realm of our total existence, whether we are unborn, a young woman in the prime of her life, or an old man on his deathbed. To destroy human life is a crime against God and a rejection of the truth that we were made in His image.

Throughout the Bible, God has plenty to say about the taking of human life. Most people in our nation, though they may not be familiar with all of the Ten Commandments know that "Thou Shalt Not Kill" is listed. Everything in the universe belongs to God. Psalm 24:1 says: *"The earth is the LORD's, and all its fullness, the world and those who dwell therein."* Our own lives are a precious gift given to us but ultimately we belong to God! We are His possessions; we have only been granted stewardship over our lives and the earth we live on. Though children pass through us, they are not ours, any more than we are property of our parents. Psalm 127:3 says: *"Behold, children are a heritage from the LORD, the fruit of the womb is a reward."* The fetal tissue in the womb is a child and it is a gift from God. Each of us has been given the gift of life and freedom for which we are responsible and accountable to God. None of us has the right to deny that same gift to an unborn person. It is an honor to carry that powerful force of another life within our very bodies, a life made in the very image of God! God has a plan and a purpose for everyone from the beginning of time and we must not do anything that will oppose His Will. We need to turn from our heartlessness and defend the sanctity of human life! Out of respect for God, let us offer mercy and compassion to every life around us, born or unborn. Let us give life instead of taking life away. Our country goes along its way, leaving lawmakers to decide how the slaughter should continue. We have bought into the lie and another deception that those we get rid of are not real people. We should be able to see through it by now but as usual, most of us let circumstances and the current way dictate to us what is acceptable or not. Proverbs 24:11-12 says: *"Deliver those who are drawn toward death, and hold back those stumbling to the slaughter. If you say, 'Surely we did not know this,' does not He who weighs the hearts consider it? He who keeps your soul, does He not know it? And will He not render to each man according to his deeds?"*

There are too many of us who prefer to let the media do our thinking for us. If we disagree, many of us are too intimidated to ever speak out with conviction. As we let time go by, our godly convictions begin to slip away. We are all accountable to God, not only for our individual lives, but also as a nation.

If you are one that has had an abortion, realize that God still loves you and He will forgive you. Free yourself from the anxiety of believing that God will not. Genuinely come to Jesus Christ, ask Him for forgiveness and surrender your life to Him.

I am concerned of what my family and friends will think of me and what they will say if I preach God's Word to them. How would I go about being a good ambassador of God?

Matthew 5:11-12 says: *"Blessed are you when they revile and persecute you, and say all kinds of evil against you falsely for My sake. Rejoice and be exceedingly glad, for great is your reward in heaven, for so they persecuted the prophets who were before you."*

If you truly accepted Jesus Christ, you will want God's Word to get out to the world. You will feel the passion for Christ and the love of the Holy Spirit being poured out upon you and you would want others to feel that as well. So share the good news of the gospel. Have you ever not been excited and could not wait to tell a friend your good news about a job promotion or any other good news that you may have had? You should feel the same way about the gospel and be excited to share it with others, because the gospel and your new life in Christ is the best news that you can ever share! If you are excited to tell people about all of your good news, then why would you want to keep the best news that you have ever received to yourself? The best thing about this great news as opposed to other great news that you may have received is that when you tell people this great news of the gospel, everyone can benefit from it. Understand that part of being a good ambassador of God is to tell people about His Word; do not keep it to yourself. 2 Corinthians 5:20 says: *"Now then, we are ambassadors for Christ, as though God were pleading through us: we implore you on Christ's behalf, be reconciled to God."* It is not only the job of spiritual leaders to teach God's Word but it is also the job of all who He calls on. He uses ordinary people like you and I so realize that God has called you to seek the lost. We are here to accomplish one thing, and that is we are to be witnesses of Jesus Christ, and we are to be salt and light. God wants the gospel to get out to mankind in order to save them from their sins. He also tells us in the Bible to go out into the world to preach His Word making disciples of all nations. Matthew 28:19-20 says: *"Go therefore and make disciples of all the nations, baptizing them in the name of the Father and of the Son and of the Holy Spirit, teaching them to observe all things that I have commanded you; and lo, I am with you always, even to the end of the age."* Amen. Do not be ashamed to speak His Word because of what people may think of you. Matthew 10:32 says: *"Therefore whoever confesses Me before men, him I will also confess before My Father who is in heaven."* Do not fear rejection and let the approval of man become more important to you than the approval of God. Also remember that other people's opinions of you are not nearly as important as God's opinion of you. Choose to live to please God not people. By choosing to please God we need to help and minister to those in need of the truth in their lives and in turn that will please God, because that is what He wants us to do. We need to nurture people with His Word. That is His Will and it is no secret. So do not fear and be ashamed to spread the testimony of our Lord and Savior Jesus Christ. 2 Timothy 1:7-9 says: *"For God has not given us a spirit of fear, but of power and of love and of a sound mind. Therefore do not be ashamed of the testimony of our Lord, nor of me His prisoner, but share with me in the sufferings for the gospel according to the power of God, who has saved us and called us with a holy calling, not according to our works, but according to His own purpose and grace which was given to us in Christ Jesus before time began."*

Now I would like to ask you, would you rather have your family, friends, and others lose their soul because you are concerned of what they will think of you and what they might say about you? I believe that you would not want that. Whether people realize it or not, you are helping them come to eternal salvation and you are helping them open their eyes to the truth. For some, you may be the last chance they have to see the light. They will be more than grateful to you once they notice what you have done for them. It is an unsurpassed feeling when you have turned someone towards Christ. People need to know about Jesus Christ and if you do not say anything, how are they going to have a chance to know Him? You will actually be doing them much harm if you do not tell them about Christ and you will not be helping yourself either. God does not want anyone left in the dark. He wants everyone to be aware of the consequences of sin so that we can live a righteous, peaceful, and prosperous life and most importantly, be eternally saved. It is very important that you share His Word and you can simply start by sharing your testimony of what your life was like before Jesus and what it has been like since Jesus has changed your life. You will see that God will takeover from there. Ask God for boldness and courage to step out in your faith so you can tell others about His undying love for mankind. However, recognize that salvation of souls is

God's territory and He works in countless ways to reach the unsaved. Many followers of God are pressured into feeling they are responsible for every unsaved person and that they are God's only instrument to reach everyone possible out there. God will use you as an instrument to reach the ones He directs you to speak with and His words will flow from you. When this happens, there is no pressure and no effort because the Holy Spirit is the One doing all the work and He is just moving through you. The Spirit of God will testify on your behalf and will not leave you on your own, so do not be concerned. Matthew 10:19-20 says: *"...do not worry about how or what you should speak. For it will be given to you in that hour what you should speak; for it is not you who speak, but the Spirit of your Father who speaks in you."* The Holy Spirit will speak the truth through you to someone, and God will lead you to the person that you are to speak to or He will lead them to you. You will know and you will be excited when He has presented the opportunity for you to speak. When you release the responsibility of witnessing into God's hands, you will be pleasantly surprised at how He will work through you. It will result in joy as you will discover that when you are witnessing to someone, it will serve as a dual purpose. Not only will you be planting a seed, but you will also keep learning and growing spiritually, and be encouraged as well.

God wants people to come to Him of their own free will and people need to know the truth so that they can make the right decision in their lives. But when you do speak the truth, do not lash out or force it on a person, instead speak God's Word and answer them in love and grace. Colossians 4:6 says: *"Let your speech always be with grace, seasoned with salt, that you may know how you ought to answer each one."* Remember that you cannot change anyone so do not become discouraged, annoyed, or angry if the person you are speaking to is not ready to hear the truth or just simply does not believe. Your job is only to plant the seed of the gospel and pray that they to come to the truth. In the end it is only up to the person that hears the gospel to desire to change and accept it. But you must understand that you do need to rebuke with all authority. Rebuke meaning to speak the truth in love by warning in a loving, but powerful and authoritative manner — to call to one's attention some mistake or error so that person may avoid that error in the future. We need to rebuke for the purpose of correction so people can see the real danger of sin. We are to proclaim what God's Word says about sin. 2 Timothy 4:2 says: *"Preach the word!*

Be ready in season and out of season. Convince, rebuke, exhort, with all longsuffering and teaching." We are to judge sin, but always with the goal of presenting the solution for sin and its consequences. If someone comes against you when you are trying to help them come to Christ, do not get in a foolish dispute with them because disputes are useless. Be kind and walk away from the dispute. Titus 3:9-11 says: *"But avoid foolish disputes, genealogies, contentions, and strivings about the law; for they are unprofitable and useless. Reject a divisive man after the first and second admonition, knowing that such a person is warped and sinning, being self-condemned."*

You should not only speak God's word but entirely let your whole attitude show that you are of God — live the truth. Be a reflection of Christ — let your actions speak the truth. Matthew 5:16 says: *"Let your light so shine before men, that they may see your good works and glorify your Father in heaven."* Many people may speak the truth but it is not followed up by their actions. So ask God to purify your motives so you will speak and act in the right way for the right reasons, only to please God and to bless others. Resist the lies of the world and ask God to help you always follow His truth and speak the truth in love. Let the Holy Spirit continue to transform you as you keep yourself from being polluted by worldly principles and possessions. It is God's gracious law and treasures of His Spirit that we must focus on, which truly set us free.

God's true people are of love, understanding, patience, gentleness, and kindness. Do not lay judgment upon people or you will be judged by God. Matthew 7:1 says: *"Judge not, that you be not judged."* Genuinely forgive one another like God has forgiven you. Colossians 3:13 says: *"...bearing with one another, and forgiving one another, if anyone has a complaint against another; even as Christ forgave you, so you also must do."* Continue to forgive no matter how many times a person sins against you. Matthew 18:21-22 says: *Then Peter came to Him and said, "Lord, how often shall my brother sin against me, and I forgive him? Up to seven times?" Jesus said to him, "I do not say to you, up to seven times, but up to seventy times seven.* Be willing to let go of any grudges that you might be holding against someone and you must overcome any feelings of hate, anger, and bitterness. Romans 12:14 says: *"Bless those who persecute you; bless and do not curse."* Grudges put you in the worst possible bondage imaginable and if you forgive or you ask for forgiveness, you will feel as if a weight has been lifted off of your chest! Forgive anyone that has hurt you and cancel any debt that someone owes you — meaning that you decide not to hold anything against the offending person. Extend mercy and grace to others when they make mistakes and forgive no matter the situation. Romans 12:17 says: *"Repay no one evil for evil."* If you are willing to let go from all that you are holding onto, God will soften your heart and provide you the freedom and the peace that you need to free yourself from your anger and bitterness. Yet by making the first move and asking the person that you are holding a grudge against to forgive you, you will actually be freeing yourself of that grudge. Not only that, but oftentimes when that kind act is performed you will make that person free themselves of their anger and bitterness as well. Ephesians 4:31-32 says: *"Let all bitterness, wrath, anger, clamor, and evil speaking be put away from you, with all malice. And be kind to one another, tenderhearted, forgiving one another, even as God in Christ forgave you."* Matthew 5:44-45 says: *"But I say to you, love your enemies, bless those who curse you, do good to those who hate you, and pray for those who spitefully use you and persecute you, that you may be sons of your Father in heaven; for He makes His sun rise on the evil and on the good, and sends rain on the just and on the unjust."* To love and to forgive is the only way that we will overcome Satan's infectious attitude of hate, anger, and bitterness. Romans 12:21 says: *"Do not be overcome by evil, but overcome evil with good."* Ephesians 4:26-27 says: *"...do not let the sun go down on your wrath, nor give place to the devil."* Also keep in mind that by being loving and forgiving and asking people to forgive you of anything, you are actually serving and honoring God in the process. So keep doing what is right, regardless of how people respond, and know that God notices and will bless you for your efforts.

Do not point your finger or accuse anyone. Instead, go out and be a good influence and help people with the love that God has given you, and in turn, God will help you. Continue to encourage people and let the Spirit of God shine through you to reflect God's love toward others. Set an example in speech, in life, and in love. Always humble yourself and clothe yourself in humility. Do not come across as being better than everyone else and do not look for prestige or honor when you are recognized. Be well disciplined and righteous. Those are the kind of people of whom God is looking for to build His Kingdom with. You should be quick to listen, slow to speak, and slow to become angry, for a person's anger does not bring about the righteous life that God desires. Pray for the Holy Spirit to continue to guide you as you are growing in Christ. Always glorify God in what you say, your actions, and your decisions because you want people to see through you His goodness and His selfless loving ways. You must always speak the truth and everything you do is to be done out of love because we are all brothers and sisters in Christ. Ephesians 4:25 says: *Therefore, putting away lying, "Let each one of you speak truth with his neighbor," for we are members of one another.* 1 Corinthians 16:14 says: *"Let all that you do be done with love."* As Jesus Christ is enough for you in your life, through your example, others will come to recognize that Christ is enough for them in their life as well, and need nothing more.

Be careful of your tongue because it is a world of evil among the parts of the body and it will corrupt you. Think twice before you speak. If you consider being of God and you do not keep a tight rein on your tongue, you will deceive yourself and your relationship will be worthless. Ephesians 4:29 says: *"Let no corrupt word proceed out of your mouth, but what is good for necessary edification, that it may impart grace to the hearers."* Do not swear when you speak. Let your yes be yes and your no be no. Speak and act as those who are going to be judged by the law that gives freedom because judgment without mercy will be shown to anyone who has not been merciful.

Do not show favoritism for the rich over the poor or any type of favoritism, for the Lord shows no favoritism. James 2:1-9 says: *"My brethren, do not hold the faith of our Lord Jesus Christ, the Lord of glory, with partiality. For if there should come into your assembly a man with gold rings, in fine apparel, and there should also come in a poor man in filthy clothes, and you pay attention to the one wearing the fine clothes and say to him, 'You sit here in a good place,' and say to the poor man, 'You stand there,' or, 'Sit here at my footstool,' have you not shown partiality among yourselves, and become judges with evil thoughts? Listen, my beloved brethren: Has God not chosen the poor of this world to be rich in faith and heirs of the kingdom which He promised to those who love Him? But you have dishonored the poor man. Do not the rich oppress you and drag you into the courts? Do they not blaspheme that noble name by which you are called? If you really fulfill the royal law according to the Scripture, 'You shall love your neighbor as yourself,' you do well; but if you show partiality, you commit sin, and are convicted by the law as transgressors."*

You need not to boast about tomorrow because you do not know what tomorrow brings. Only if it is God's Will, then you will do what you have planned. Proverbs 27:1 says *"Do not boast about tomorrow, For you do not know what a day may bring forth."* James 4:13-15 says: *Come now, you who say, "Today or tomorrow we will go to such and such a city, spend a year there, buy and sell, and make a profit"; whereas you do not know what will happen tomorrow. For what is your life? It is even a vapor that appears for a little time and then vanishes away. Instead you ought to say, "If the Lord wills, we shall live and do this or that."*

When God blesses you do not glory in yourself. Be humble and give Him the glory because every good and perfect gift is from above. *1* Corinthians 1:31 says: *that, as it is written, "He who glories, let him glory in the LORD."* James 1:17 says: *"Every good gift and every perfect gift is from above, and comes down from the Father of lights, with whom there is no variation or shadow of turning."* Do not let your pride take over and brag about your riches and that you have accomplished things on your own because it states in Deuteronomy 8:18: *"And you shall remember the Lord your God, for it is He who gives you power to get wealth."*

Thank God for everything that you have and everything that you have accomplished.

If you turn a sinner from the error of their way, you will save them from death and cover over a multitude of sins. But a person who hears the Word of the Lord that you have preached and does not put them into practice is a foolish and unwise person. Luke 6:49 says: *"But he who heard and did nothing is like a man who built a house on the earth without a foundation, against which the stream beat vehemently; and immediately it fell. And the ruin of that house was great."* Anyone then who knows the truth and the good they ought to do and does not do it, is a sinner. Hebrews 10:26-27 says: *"For if we sin willfully after we have received the knowledge of the truth, there no longer remains a sacrifice for sins, but a certain fearful expectation of judgment, and fiery indignation which will devour the adversaries."* A fearful expectation of judgment and of raging fire will consume the enemies of God.

Be an imitator of God, walk in His light, understand and accomplish His Will, speak the truth in love, and you will be a good ambassador. Ephesians 5:1-5 says: *"Therefore be imitators of God as dear children. And walk in love, as Christ also has loved us and given Himself for us, an offering and a sacrifice to God for a sweet-smelling aroma. But fornication and all uncleanness or covetousness, let it not even be named among you, as is fitting for saints; neither filthiness, nor foolish talking, nor coarse jesting, which are not fitting, but rather giving of thanks. For this you know, that no fornicator, unclean person, nor covetous man, who is an idolater, has any inheritance in the kingdom of Christ and God."* Ephesians 5:8-17 says: *"For you were once darkness, but now you are light in the Lord. Walk as children of light (for the fruit of the Spirit is in all goodness, righteousness, and truth), finding out what is acceptable to the Lord. And have no fellowship with the unfruitful works of darkness, but rather expose them. For it is shameful even to speak of those things which are done by them in secret. But all things that are exposed are made manifest by the light, for whatever makes manifest is light. Therefore He says: "Awake, you who sleep, Arise from the dead, And Christ will give you light." See then that you walk circumspectly, not as fools but as wise, redeeming the time, because the days are evil. Therefore do not be unwise, but understand what the will of the Lord is.*

God also wants you to bear much fruit in life. If you abide in Christ and disconnect yourself with worldly desires and follow His righteous ways, then you will bear much Godly fruit. In turn, all the fruit that you do produce will glorify God and you will indeed be a disciple of Christ. The souls that will be saved, which you helped bring toward God and come to faith in Christ because of your ministry, will be your fruit! John 15:8 says: *"By this My Father is glorified, that you bear much fruit; so you will be My disciples."* It is surreal to be a disciple of Jesus Christ! By being a true disciple, God will bless you for the work that you do and that you have done for Him in sharing His Word with others. Hebrews 6:10 says: *"For God is not unjust to forget your work and labor of love which you have shown toward His name, in that you have ministered to the saints, and do minister."* God will make you a blessing to your family, your friends, and to others. People will see a big difference in you as you continue to let the Holy Spirit radiate through you and He will let your good works of your ministry shine. May you be light in dark places!

How do we know that God really exists and that He is our creator?

Genesis 1:1 says: *In the beginning God created the heavens and the earth.* We complicate things that are so obvious and all that we have to do is to stop playing these games and start opening our eyes! We need to start believing and give faith a chance. The only two choices that we can choose from are revelation and speculation. We can believe that God is our creator and did create the universe, thus believing the gospel or we can believe that everything just happened by chance and perfectly came to be from nothing. How can we possibly make sense out of nobody times nothing equals everything, which is the way of evolution? It would actually take more faith to believe in evolution than creation. Genesis 2:7 says: *"...And the LORD God formed man of the dust of the ground, and breathed into his nostrils the breath of life; and man became a living being."* Genesis 2:21-22 says: *"...And the LORD God caused a deep sleep to fall on Adam, and he slept; and He took one of his ribs, and closed up the flesh in its place. Then the rib which the LORD God had taken from man He made into a woman, and He brought her to the man."* We are not an accident and to believe that is very shameful. We have meaning to our existence. What is the purpose of living this life if there is nothing else after we pass? It seems like a great deal of trouble to go through for nothing. The theory of evolution is without doubt another masterminded deception of Satan. He has many people believing in evolution and because of evolution, we do not need a creator and therefore, there is no one that we have to answer to when we pass from this physical life, so we do not have to worry about being eternally punished for our sins, thus we continue on sinning, which results in a fallen self-centered world as Satan desires it to be. We must remember that Satan opposes God's rule through mans affairs and he has influence over all who do not believe and lack faith in God and His Son Jesus Christ.

Charles Darwin was proven wrong on all levels and it has been confirmed many times over that the theory of evolution is a fallacy. Evolution fails to provide answers. It has many holes in it that it is a sinking ship. People are told that evolution produced all of our life forms. But it is not told that scientists themselves have gradually, over the years, abandoned one after another, the various means—the mechanisms by which evolution could occur and all the mechanisms of evolution that have been disproved and discarded have been by reputable scientists. If we can believe in Charles Darwin's existence to be true from only trusting and believing in what the history books say, then why can we not believe in God's existence to be true from the best historical book that was ever written (the Bible)? In fact, such historical accuracy is what you would expect of a book inspired by God. So what then makes only Charles Darwin's existence to be true and not God's? If the human race is the most intelligent creature on earth, then why do we even give the idea of evolution a chance? We must not feed into Satan and let him influence us with all his lies. If we are truly intelligent then it would only make sense to believe in a creator. Psalm 53:1 says: *The fool has said in his heart, "There is no God."* There is no other explanation how all things were made, including the universe, heaven, and earth. Psalm 121:2 says: *"My help comes from the LORD, Who made heaven and earth."*

The complexity of our planet points to a purposeful and an intelligent Designer who not only created our universe, but sustains it today. We need to look beyond our physical eyes and having faith will give you the wisdom and enlightenment to know God personally. Trust the Bible and you will find your answer. It is not surprising that scientists and doctors everywhere are turning to God because there are things that even they cannot explain. Science is increasingly showing that our universe has been created by a creator. Without God science is of no use because He created science and has given us science as a tool in order to prove His existence. In fact, science has recently proven that the centuries old shroud of Turin, which bears the image of our crucified Christ, was discovered to be authentic. Scientists have used today's technology of a scanner and have said, "That the only way the image could have been engraved into the shroud was by light, which is the exact same way that a scanner produces images. The only thing is that there was no technology of that type back then. Therefore, it could have not been done by a scanner." They said that, "Much research and many years of hard work has been done on the shroud and there is no other explanation other than light that could have created the image." It was then said, and I truly believe and completely trust to be true, "The only possibility in which the image could have been created was by the light that came from the glory of the direct result of the resurrection of Jesus Christ." It was left for mankind as a part of proof of His existence. Scientists then proceeded to put the face of the image in a three dimensional view and showed the markings that were engraved on the images forehead, and associated them with the wounds from the crown that was put on Christ's head when He was tortured. They also then went on to prove the markings of the severely battered body that were engraved on the back and front side of the shroud with their technology. From the nail wounds in Christ's hands and feet, to the severe flogging on His back and neck, to the bruised shoulders when He was carrying the cross. The Scientists were in awe in all of this and then finally acknowledged that it <u>MOST CETRTAINLY</u> is the image of Christ on the centuries old shroud of Turin.

Scientists for many years have been trying to prove that God does not exist but could never explain the unexplainable because it is Jesus Christ who has disproved the laws of science when He was born of a virgin, when He feed the five thousand with two fish and five loaves of bread, when he ascended into heaven, when He cured the blind and sick without any medicine, and when He rose from the dead. God is still performing miracles today and therefore, He is the only way that we can explain the unexplainable. Miracles are outside the bounds of science, outside the bounds of logic, and outside the bounds of reason. Science can never explain why when it comes to the unexplainable and it is because miracles can only be explained by way of a divine origin. If man stood on the Word of God they would be able to explain the unexplainable and they would see miracles all around them, all the time.

The truth is that we know God exists because He appeared in human flesh. 1 Timothy 3:16 says: *"...God was manifested in the flesh."* Jesus Christ was God Almighty who became man and it is clear that Jesus came to earth to reveal who God is to mankind and what He is all about. Jesus performing miracles, healing people and rising from the dead established Himself as having the credentials to be God and it was these facts that demonstrated its truth to the unbelieving world. Jesus Christ and the Bible are two powerful reasons that God does exist. God does not force us to believe in Him because of free will, but He could. Instead, He has provided sufficient proof of His existence for us to willingly respond to Him. For example the earth's perfect distance from the sun, the unique chemical properties of water, and many unbelievers all over the world have turned from their ways and have come to faith and have shared it through their testimonies. I have come across unbelievers who have now come to faith in Christ and they have all said, that they did not realize that the reason the subject of God weighed so heavily on their minds was because it was God who was pushing the issue. They could not break free of thinking about the possibility of God. They have said that, "God wants to be known and that He has created us with the intent that we would know Him and we would know Him through Jesus Christ, because He is the clearest and most specific picture of God." They have also said, "If truth be told, He has surrounded us with much evidence of Himself and He keeps the question of His existence directly before us." The former nonbelievers have also stated that, "The underlying reason why unbelievers are bothered with people who believe in God is because God endlessly pursues them. But it is for the reason that He desires to seek out and save the lost." We cannot deny the evidence of God's existence because it is all around us — the many people who attest to knowing God, unexplainable experience's — miracles, the gnawing in our hearts and minds to determine if God exists, and the willingness for God to be known through Jesus Christ. More proof of the living Almighty God would be all of His creatures that have their own incredible unique abilities and survival methods. Their own perfectly designed unique ways about them can teach us and tell us that they were designed by God. Job 12:7, 10 says: *"But now ask the beasts, and they will teach you; And the birds of the air, and they will tell you." "In whose hand is the life of every living thing, And the breath of all mankind?"* God has also designed every living thing to change and adapt so it can survive the constantly changing environment — not evolution. Finally, I would also like to add the sophistication of the human mind and body, and the complexity and preciseness of the human DNA in our cells.

The human DNA is more complex than anything that was ever put together. It by far surpasses anything that any human can ever think of and it is unfathomable by even mankind's greatest mind. It was stated by Bill Gates founder of Microsoft that "DNA is like a software program, only much more complex than anything we've ever devised." It was discovered that the human DNA is made up of billions of genetic letters and are all amazingly in proper sequence. It was found that DNA is actually embedded with information. It provides detailed instructions for assembling proteins and how the person's body should develop in the form of a four character digital code. You cannot find instruction, precise information like this, without someone intentionally creating it. The information that is stored in our DNA is comparable to several sets of encyclopedias. There is a universe inside a single cell and the human body has trillions of cells that carry the DNA digital code.

Now could evolution have come up with such miniaturized information and have placed this massive amount of genetic letters in one cell and in their appropriate order? Not to mention the fact that trillions of cells in our body carry the DNA digital code, let alone one. Every detail is perfectly designed and this superior level of information is an intelligent design and could only have come from an intelligent Designer — God. Evolution is a myth and the evidence clearly points to it. How can such a perfectly designed creation just evolve? Let us give God the credit! Romans 1:20 says: *"For since the creation of the world His invisible attributes are clearly seen, being understood by the things that are made, even His eternal power and Godhead, so that they (people) are without excuse."*

From my experiences alone, I can honestly say that God does without a doubt exist. He is the greatest example of love, grace, hope, forgiveness, peace, patience and true kindness. Since accepting Jesus Christ on a personal level, being obedient and giving faith a chance, all of God's promises that He declares in His Word (the Bible) have come true for me. We should not deny our own creator, but rather seek

Him out, open our hearts, and give Him a chance to come into our lives. You too will experience the promises that God declares for you in His Word (the Bible), if you give him a chance and trust in Him. *Deuteronomy 7:9 says: "Therefore know that the LORD your God, He is God, the faithful God who keeps covenant and mercy for a thousand generations with those who love Him and keep His commandments."* The only regret that I have is that I did not come to Christ sooner. The Holy Spirit pours out from me and I can never get enough of God. Faith in Christ has opened my eyes as it will yours! The supernatural power of the gospel is incredibly amazing to those who put their faith in it and live by it! The Bible has all of the answers to life!

Why is money considered the root of all evil when we need it to live?

Money is not evil; it is the love of money that is a root of all evil. 1 Timothy 6:10 says: *"For the love of money is a root of all kinds of evil."* Sadly, people will do anything in the name of money. Many are highly motivated by it and are controlled by it. The love of money creates greed and people's lies and dishonesty to obtain money is motivated by their greed to become wealthy. The love of money is the reason why much of it is ill-gained and therefore, brings much corruption and crisis to the world. Many have developed a fondness for money and have greedily devoted themselves to the accumulation of riches, and eventually it will lead and it has led to their inevitable end. Proverbs 1:19 says: *"So are the ways of everyone who is greedy for gain; It takes away the life of its owners."* 1 Timothy 6:9 says: *"But those who desire to be rich fall into temptation and a snare, and into many foolish and harmful lusts which drown men in destruction and perdition."* Many who have become slaves of money and many who have desired to be rich, have reaped tragic consequences.

The love of money has also been the culprit of many family feuds and friendship arguments and has torn them apart. Yet again, we let Satan influence us and we believe the deception that money is everything and sadly, we are willing to destroy our families and friendships over it, exactly as Satan wishes. We must stop following his ways of destruction. The love of money is indeed a root of all evil things and it will become your master if you let it. The struggle to get it and keep it allows time for nothing else. We need to pursue more important things in life, such as a close bond with God, family and friends. Keep money in its place. Survey after survey shows that those who care more about people than they do about money are happier. We should also be aware of whatever money God may bless us with that is beyond our daily needs, we ought to make use of it according to His will and not our own. We also need to see that there are blessings greater than material riches. Material wealth does not lead to happiness. If you put money first in your life before God it then becomes an idol of worship, it is idolatry and you are worshipping the created things and not your creator. Money will not always be there for you and will not lead to happiness. On the other hand God will always be there for you.

True happiness and the true riches are the things that have eternal value and are found in Jesus Christ.

Living by the principles of the Bible opens up so many blessings in life, such as a happier marriage, peace of mind no matter the circumstance, a good conscience, real joy and fulfillment, and a healthier stress free life. Spiritual riches are much more valuable than any material riches. We can only find true and lasting happiness after we properly satisfy our spiritual needs. If we put Jesus Christ in our lives first, we will find that every aspect of our lives becomes richer and more rewarding.

The love of money does create greed and thankfully, we can say that money will not always be a cause for concern. The Bible assures us of a future when greedy and exploitive commerce will be permanently removed. God's new system of things that follows will be governed by His righteous principles. The earth will be transformed into a paradise as God originally purposed it to be. It will be a blessing to see the entire earth filled with happiness, peace and love! It will be unlike anything humanity has ever known. Life at that time will be incredible as God fulfills His original purpose for mankind. People will live life the way God actually intended it to be lived and we will have that intimate relationship with our own creator. Everyone who sincerely exercises faith in Jesus Christ will not be disappointed. How wise, therefore, would it be to pursue the things of the spirit rather than the materialism of this world!

How does God speak to us and how does He answer our prayers?

It is very important that we listen to God when He speaks to us. He speaks to us in many ways. Most importantly we need to listen to what God says when He speaks to us through the Bible. We can know and have assurance that the Word of God (the Bible), is how God talks to us. We need to stop wondering how God speaks to us and recognize that He has spoken to us through the Bible. In the Bible God has given us all things that pertain to life and what we need to do. We do not need anything else from God. We have all we need in the Bible to live prosperously, productively, and peacefully — to live a faithful life in the Lord. Timothy 3:16-17 says: *"All Scripture is given by inspiration of God, and is profitable for doctrine, for reproof, for correction, for instruction in righteousness, that the man of God may be complete, thoroughly equipped for every good work."* The Bible is our lifeline and blueprint that guides us through life. It is God's law book to humanity and through its scripture God speaks to us. In God's Word, we find His thoughts, wisdom, knowledge, and ideas and as we study it, meditate on it and believe, they become ingrained in us.

Once we have committed our lives to Jesus Christ, the Holy Spirit dwelling within us will help us to remember the Word of God and apply it when we need it. As you are reading the Bible God will sometimes cause certain scriptures to stand out at particular times.

When we pray with faith, by God's good grace He can additionally lead us to different types of media to find the answers to our prayers as well, such as newspapers, books, movies, music, television, radio, etc. God can also speak to us and answer us through our dreams and we can also find our answers through others that God leads us to. God is in many places and by having faith it makes Him very easy to be found. Without faith however, we will fail to notice His warnings and fail to recognize when He has answered us. By faith and studying God's Word (the Bible), you will know and have no doubt when that moment has come when He has given you confirmation or has revealed to you your answer. When you are faithful in Christ things will no longer feel like a coincidence to you. You will realize without a doubt that what you thought were coincidences before is truly God speaking to us. For example, God bringing the right people into your life at your lowest point to help you get through your adversities, God putting together all the right people in your life to help you accomplish His purpose, being at the right place at the right time, God bringing new people into your life and God bringing past people back into your life unexpectedly because they are all in need of the gospel and God knows that you will be willing to share it with them, now that you have come to faith. You have learned to acknowledge His miracles because of your faith, and you now know that it was a miracle from God that has brought you to Him and has saved you. You have realized that He has planned your salvation before you were born because He knew you were willing to be saved. You have realized it was Him that has orchestrated His Will in your life and has revealed your spiritual gifts so you can complete His purpose, and it was not coincidental. Whatever it may be, with faith in Christ you will have no doubt when something is from Him and not coincidental. On the other hand the unbelievers fail to recognize when He is speaking to them and fail to recognize His gracious warnings over and over again, until eventually it may sadly be too late. One example is Christ bringing the gospel to them over many years through by different means, including visions and dreams but they continue to simply ignore it. Each time they could not care less because they are just plain ignorant about the fact that it may be God speaking

261

to them. For the unbeliever their understanding is darkened because they have hardened their heart and what they believe are coincidences, is in actuality God letting them know that He does exist, so that they have the chance to turn from his or her wrong and futile ways and be eternally saved. There are no coincidences with our Lord and Savior.

You must also be aware that Satan can also speak to us. But once again with faith, God will make things stand out and feel right when it is He that has led you. Always ask God to make you aware of all things that are of Him.

Why do I not understand the way of God?

Matthew 6:22-23 says: *"The lamp of the body is the eye. If therefore your eye is good, your whole body will be full of light. But if your eye is bad, your whole body will be full of darkness. If therefore the light that is in you is darkness, how great is that darkness!"* We do not fully understand God's ways because we do not see the big picture. Humanity is deceived into believing it is all about the here and now and our minds are of this world. We are conformed to this world and therefore, we are spiritually dead, causing our understanding to be darkened to the very importance of God's perfect Will, eternity, and the true meaning of life. Romans 12:2 says: *"And do not be conformed to this world, but be transformed by the renewing of your mind, that you may prove what is that good and acceptable and perfect will of God."* By being spiritually dead we are alienated from God because He is of the spirit and as a result, we will not see the things of the spirit. We must recognize that God is preparing us for something much greater than this existence and we must wake up our soul to see it. God is of the spirit, He is infinite, and He is beyond our comprehension. Mankind is limited and not of the spirit and our only way to have a chance to understand God's ways is to look through our spiritual eyes — having faith. 1 Corinthians 2:14 says: *"But the natural man does not receive the things of the Spirit of God, for they are foolishness to him; nor can he know them, because they are spiritually discerned."* We do not fully understand God's ways because God looks at things from a holy, spiritual, and eternal perspective. Mankind looks at things from a sinful, earthly, and temporal perspective. Isaiah 55:8-9 says: *"For My thoughts are not your thoughts, nor are your ways My ways," says the LORD. "For as the heavens are higher than the earth, so are My ways higher than your ways, and My thoughts than your thoughts."* God's ways are much greater because He looks at the whole picture — eternity. He desires to save our soul because He does not wish for any of His children to suffer eternally in hell. It is not our physical being that God worries as much about because our bodies are just a shell that is only temporal and it will soon pass. But it is His true children's precious soul that matters most to God because the soul is the essence of our being, and it is what suffers eternal death or lives on forever with God after this life has passed. Our eternal destiny depends on us and without repentance of our sins we are destined for eternal damnation. But God and His awesome grace wishes to save us from eternal destruction and that is why He has sent His only Son Jesus Christ to die on the cross for us all and to save us from our sins. Jesus Christ did all the work for us. All that we have to do is sincerely accept the free gift of salvation that God has given us through His Son Jesus and repent of our sins. It is impossible to see the way of God if we have not accepted Jesus Christ as our Lord and Savior and are not living by faith. If we lack faith in Christ then we will continue to stay spiritually dead because of our sins. Sin blinds us from seeing the things of God and only through Christ will the blindfold come off and we will then be made spiritually alive. We will now be able to see the big picture and it is only then when we are given grace, understanding of the truth, and the wisdom of God.

Once again, and I cannot stress it enough, by willingly and genuinely repenting of your sins through Jesus Christ and surrendering your life to Him, He will cleanse you of all your sins. At last, the Holy Spirit will waken your soul and will allow you to see how immoral your sin is and turn you away from it. The Spirit of God will begin to spiritually transform your mind and will now permit you to see through the eyes of God. Through your transformation by the Holy Spirit, God will start to finally reveal Himself to you. You will finally see God's ways and have His wisdom and understand His glorious and amazing plan of eternal salvation. It is remarkable to see God's Will unfold before your eyes!

Seek true change in your life. God has a great purpose for you and wants to help you grow as a person. Invite Jesus into your life and let God lead you toward the best life possible and transform you into the person He wants you to become. Ask God to help you be patient as He renews your mind and transforms your life. Replace wrong thoughts that you may have about God with thoughts that line up with the Bible's truth. As the Holy Spirit guides you, you will gain the confidence you need to trust Him more as He changes you.

Is there life after death?
Should I fear dying?

There is much fear in the minds of many concerning what awaits us at the time of our death. But God's true word claims that death was once conquered. The good news is that Jesus Christ, the resurrected One has defeated death forever. He said that He would rise again after three days and so He did. Matthew 20:18-19 says: *"Behold, we are going up to Jerusalem, and the Son of Man will be betrayed to the chief priests and to the scribes; and they will condemn Him to death, and deliver Him to the Gentiles to mock and to scourge and to crucify. And the third day He will rise again."* Acts 10:40-41 says: *"…Him God raised up on the third day, and showed Him openly, not to all the people, but to witnesses chosen before by God, even to us who ate and drank with Him after He arose from the dead."* He also said that His children would have life after death and that is the reason why Jesus has sacrificed Himself — to give us everlasting life. If you believe that Christ rose from the dead and can raise others as well, then that will help you let go of the bondage of the fear of death that Satan is subjecting you to and therefore, you can live in peace concerning death.

The knowledge and wisdom of Jesus will deliver His children from the bondage of fear to a life of peace. Hebrews 2:14-15 says: *"...He Himself likewise shared in the same, that through death He might destroy him who had the power of death, that is, the devil, and release those who through fear of death were all their lifetime subject to bondage."*

If you know what Jesus did and what He has yet promised to do, you will find relief from your fears concerning death. God's children can enter death's door knowing that Christ has conquered death. Through the knowledge of Christ and His promises, a life without fear of death can be experienced in this world because through His death and resurrection He has defeated death, and through Him eternal life waits for us in a world to come. It is abundantly clear that death is not truly death to God's children. Jesus has abolished death for His faithful followers and has brought the understanding of this continuous existence of a life and immortality to our understanding through the good news of the gospel.

God has spelled out in His Word (the Bible), many times regarding His promise of eternal salvation. We must be aware that there <u>MOST CERTAINLY</u> is life after death and the most important thing we can do in our life is to be prepared for it by having Jesus Christ in our lives. Death is a part of life and we must all die physically because of sin that came upon the world through Adam. But we were all made alive again through Christ. 1 Corinthians 15:19-22 says: *"If in this life only we have hope in Christ, we are of all men the most pitiable. But now Christ is risen from the dead, and has become the firstfruits of those who have fallen asleep. For since by man came death, by Man also came the resurrection of the dead. For as in Adam all die, even so in Christ all shall be made alive."* We have sin and death that came through one man — Adam, but we now have forgiveness and life that came through one man — Jesus Christ, because he has defeated sin and death. That is amazing! So if we die with Christ in our lives, the true follower does not fear death because they know that Jesus has assured them eternal salvation by dying for their sins and then rising again and the Bible has many examples that provide us that comfort. John 5:24 says: *"Most assuredly, I say to you, he who hears My word and believes in Him who sent Me has everlasting life, and shall not come into judgment, but has passed from death into life."* John 11:25 says: *"Jesus said to her, 'I am the resurrection and the life. He who believes in Me, though he may die, he shall live.' "* Romans 6:8 says: *"Now if we died with Christ, we believe that we shall also live with Him, knowing that Christ, having been raised from the dead, dies no more. Death no longer has dominion over Him. For the death that He died, He died to sin once for all; but the life that He lives, He lives to God. Likewise you also, reckon yourselves to be dead indeed to sin, but alive to God in Christ Jesus our Lord."* On the other hand, if we do not have Jesus Christ in our lives, then we should certainly fear death because we have no assurance of eternal salvation and we will be separated from God forever. We will MOST DEFINITELY be destined for eternal suffering and eternal destruction. Romans 6:23 says: *"For the wages of sin is death, but the gift of God is eternal life in Christ Jesus our Lord."*

We can rejoice in Christ because His death and resurrection has secured us eternal salvation. The child of God who was given eternal life in the spiritual rebirth — the repentance of our sins and faith in Christ, retains that life; and he or she never ceases to live. The life just passes from this realm to the place where Jesus dwells. The knowledge of the passing of our lives to a better world instead of the ending of our lives sure helps us to conquer the fear of death. Near the time of Jesus' own passing He left us with these words, John 14:1-4 says: *"Let not your heart be troubled; you believe in God, believe also in Me. In My Father's house are many mansions; if it were not so, I would have told you. I go to prepare a place for you. And if I go and prepare a place for you, I will come again and receive you to Myself; that where I am, there you may be also. And where I go you know, and the way you know."* You can rest assure knowing that Christ has conquered death for His faithful followers and has given us everlasting life.

I would also like to add that by being reminded of death's reality will equip us to focus on fulfilling our true purpose for living and to live as Christ and being engaged in God's Will we have truly begun to live. I encourage you to receive God's free gift of eternal salvation while you are still on this earth because there is no chance in eternity to ever change your destiny. Isaiah 55:6 says: *"Seek the LORD while He may be found, Call upon Him while He is near."* So turn to Christ today in repentance and He will transform your life and change your eternal fate.

In addition to conquering the fear of death, by having Christ in our lives we can find much peace, comfort, and understanding in Him when going through tribulations and when a loved one has passed. It is much too difficult to get through the death of someone close to us on our own or any other circumstance on our own. Jesus is the only one that can help us heal. You can absolutely trust in Him to get you through your troubles, your pain, and your sorrow. But not only that, you will also be able to comfort others that are in need with the comfort that Christ gives you. Psalm 147:3 says: *He heals the brokenhearted And binds up their wounds.* 2 Corinthians 1:3-4 says: *"Blessed be the God and Father of our Lord Jesus Christ, the Father of mercies and God of all comfort, who comforts us in all our tribulation, that we may be able to comfort those who are in any trouble, with the comfort with which we ourselves are comforted by God."*

What are the warning signs and the scenario of the end of this age and is it drawing near? What exactly is the rapture and is it an end time event?

The evidence of the end of this age drawing near is very compelling. The Bible gives us many examples of the signs that warn us of the approaching end of the age. One example is in 2 Timothy 3:1-4: *"But know this, that in the last days perilous times will come: for men will be lovers of themselves, lovers of money, boasters, proud, blasphemers, disobedient to parents, unthankful, unholy, unloving, unforgiving, slanderers, without self-control, brutal, despisers of good, traitors, headstrong, haughty, lovers of pleasure rather than lovers of God."* Another example is stated in Daniel 12:3-5: *"But you, Daniel, shut up the words, and seal the book until the time of the end; many shall run to and fro, and knowledge shall increase."* The scripture in Daniel 12:3-5 talks about our increased knowledge in technology and we can see how it is growing more and more each and every day. Knowledge for many years was growing very slowly, but now it is growing at an unbelievable rate. It is ever more obvious that the time of God's coming is drawing near. Prophecy is being fulfilled daily and faster than ever before. Another sign we should look for is stated in Acts 2:17: *"And it shall come to pass in the last days, says God, That I will pour out of My Spirit on all flesh; Your sons and your daughters shall prophesy, Your young men shall see visions, Your old men shall dream dreams."* During the end time, God in His good grace will pour out His Holy Spirit at a faster pace and will speak to and through all who will come to Him through visions, dreams and prophecy. More people than ever before are now seeking out and coming to Jesus Christ. Another sign would be in Matthew 24:7-8 which says: *"For nation will rise against nation, and kingdom against kingdom. And there will be famines, pestilences, and earthquakes in various places. All these are the beginning of sorrows."* Another end time prophecy that is coming to pass is mentioned in Zechariah 12:2-3 which says: *"Behold, I will make Jerusalem a cup of drunkenness to all the surrounding peoples, when they lay siege against Judah and Jerusalem. And it shall happen in that day that I will make Jerusalem a very heavy stone for all peoples; all who would heave it away will surely be cut in pieces, though all nations of the earth are gathered against it.* The scripture above states that in the last day's nations will begin to oppose and burden themselves with Israel and Jerusalem and those nations will be destroyed. The prophecy of the end times predict that everything would come back around and once again be centered around Jerusalem. It has now become the center of world politics. The Bible predicts that Jerusalem will be a burdensome stone for all the nations who try to overthrow it and one nation that is burdening themselves with it and strongly desires to oppose Jerusalem and Israel is Syria. They are beginning to build and line up their arms and position themselves to invade Israel through the Golan Heights as well as from Lebanon. The scriptures states that Syria will be destroyed. Isaiah 17:1 says: *The burden against Damascus (Syria). "Behold, Damascus (Syria) will cease from being a city, And it will be a ruinous heap."* Another nation that appears to be turning on Israel is the United States. The Obama administration has decided that the real cause of America's woe is because of the support of Israel. As a result, the administration is also now, as the rest of the nations are doing and some have already done so, gradually turning their backs on their strongest allied country in the Middle East—Israel. They want Israel to surrender Jerusalem or the United States will withdraw its hand of protection from the Jewish state. But Jerusalem is in reality the heart and soul of Israel's history and Israel's claim to Jerusalem is a matter of historical fact. It is supported by the authority of the Bible itself. Also In 1995 congress passed the United States — Jerusalem act — the Jerusalem Embassy act of 1995, which legally recognized Jerusalem as Israel's capitol and provided for the relocation of the United States Embassy in Israel to Jerusalem. The Obama administration is the first administration that has ever expressed to withdraw the United States hand of protection to Israel. Why would the administration side against their strongest allied country in the Middle East over the most irrational issue? The Bible warns that the destiny of the world is inseparable from Israel and Jerusalem and that God will bless those who bless Israel and curse those who oppose Israel. God had promised Abraham in Genesis 12:3: *"I will bless those who bless you (Israel), and I will curse him who curses you (Israel); and in you (Israel) all the families of the earth shall be blessed."* The Obama administration is being manipulated and deceived and is gradually turning the United States away from a true friend — Israel, and it is a grave mistake. Unfortunately, many believe that Israel is always at fault but the truth is that Israel is the one who continually gets harassed and provoked and then gets the blame for only trying to defend itself. It does appear that the United States government may try to remove Jerusalem from Israeli control. This is very regrettable and the Bible warns of that, and it should resist such efforts wherever possible.

Satan opposes God's rule in the affairs of man and the influence and deceit that Satan has upon the nations of the world to oppose and destroy Israel — God's chosen and Promised Land to the Israelites, is clearly evident. Why else are many nations of the world gathered against it? Satan has a vendetta against God so what better satisfaction does Satan have than to oppose Israel in any way he can? Think about it! These nations of the world are being terribly deceived by another of Satan's ploys! As I already mentioned many times before, without Christ we will fall into the hands of Satan's many deceptions. We need to remember that everything in this world is influenced by the spiritual realms. Ephesians 6:12 says: *"For we do not wrestle against flesh and blood, but against principalities, against powers, against the rulers of the darkness of this age, against spiritual hosts of wickedness in the heavenly places."* The United States would rather trade the land of God's promise of peace for man's promise of peace. The world believes that if we suit the Islamists and solve the Israeli-Palestinian problem then all the other problems in the world will just simply end, but that is a deception and the complete opposite. Once again, the Bible warns and it is made very clear that Jerusalem only belongs to Israel and that there will be no peace for any nation who will continue to oppose the Israeli state and attempt to take Jerusalem away from it. The United States and Israel relations are at an all time low and many terrible events are continually happening to the United States as a result. They have turned away from the Bible and the warnings given in the scriptures are one hundred percent precise. Many will be quick to say that these events are coincidental and unrelated but how many unrelated events does it take before it becomes a pattern. With God our creator there are no coincidences. Zephaniah 3:15,19 says: *"...He has cast out your enemy. The King of Israel, the LORD, is in your midst; you shall see disaster no more ...Behold, at that time I will deal with all who afflict you."*

In the end time the United States will fade as a super power because of our failing administration due to the continued blindness and disobedience to the Word of God and will have no choice and will be forced into a one world government and economy. In reality it appears that the United States is headed that way at this present moment, because

America is currently bankrupt. Our largest states and major cities are bankrupt and as our economy fails our military will be no more. America can be forced into this type of government at any time now. As never before in history, the world's conditions are perfectly set up for the end time tribulation and the coming of the most evil dictator of all time — the Antichrist to take place, as the end time prophecies of the Bible have predicted. I will explain more on this topic, but first I would like to give explanation to the rapture before I go on and how that relates with the end time events.

Although the word rapture does not appear in the Bible the concept appears numerous times. 1 Thessalonians 4:16-17: *"For the Lord Himself will descend from heaven with a shout, with the voice of an archangel, and with the trumpet of God. And the dead in Christ will rise first. Then we who are alive and remain shall be caught up together with them in the clouds to meet the Lord in the air. And thus we shall always be with the Lord."* The already deceased who were faithful followers of Christ will rise first. Then all who are faithful followers of Jesus Christ that are still physically alive will suddenly and miraculously vanish simultaneously body and soul from the earth and their removal will be instant. Without ever experiencing death, they will be gathered up in the clouds to meet the Lord in the air and be with Him forever. Fortunately, because of the rapture all of God's children, the true followers of Christ that are still living will be saved from going through the most catastrophic and astronomical time that will ever come to pass in human history — the end time tribulation.

The reason that I say and believe that Christ's true followers will be raptured before this horrific point in time — the pre-tribulation rapture is because it would make the most sense that His true followers will not have to go through this horrendous time of great tribulation because they have believed and have trusted in Christ before hand. It is for those who did not believe in Christ before the tribulation and God is giving them one final opportunity to turn to Jesus Christ and turn from their immoral ways. The tribulation period is God's final wake up call to the world before they lose their soul and will then suffer real pain for an eternity. It is a period of time that will be so horrific and the reason being is because it is going to be a process to get the lost to respond. Anyhow, most people believe that the rapture will occur during the pre-tribulation, some believe it will happen during the mid-tribulation, and others believe it will take place during the post-tribulation. As I have mentioned, I believe the rapture will happen before the tribulation takes place because of the reason that I have already stated above and also because the end time tribulation will not occur until the Antichrist has risen and come to power and that will not happen until the followers of Christ are raptured and removed from the earth. So the main obstacle that is hindering the Antichrist from being currently revealed and marking the beginning of the tribulation is the presence of Christ's faithful followers still in the world, because it is in them that the restrainer of the Holy Spirit dwells. 2 Thessalonians 2:6-8 says: *"And now you know what is restraining, that he may be revealed in his own time. For the mystery of lawlessness is already at work; only He (the Holy Spirit) who now restrains will do so until He (the followers of Christ) is taken out of the way (raptured). And then the lawless one will be revealed."* Therefore, Christ will come and receive His children before the Antichrist's rise and reign of terror and the end time tribulation period begins. When God's church is raptured the remaining people of the world will be scrambling for answers on the disappearance of millions and they will all be told many different lies and misleading beliefs and not be told the truth of the rapture.

During the end time tribulation and another sign of the end time events, which is stated in the scriptures will be a new world order that will come about — a one global government, and a one worldwide currency, which I have already started to address. But before the new world order takes place, the United States will have to fade as a super power, which appears to be doing so and Europe will have to arise as the center of world supremacy. In addition, Christ's faithful followers will have to be raptured. When this is complete a lawless leader, a merciless dictator will rise out of the new European Union — the revived Roman Empire and new world order and will rule the world. He will be empowered by and serving Satan and will control the world and deceive many, including telling them lies of why millions have suddenly vanished from earth. This dictator will be by far worse than any dictator the world has ever seen. 1 John 2:18 says: *"Little children, it is the last hour; and as you have heard that the Antichrist is coming, even now many antichrists have come, by which we know that it is the last hour."* At first he will seem to be a savior. He will arrive as a peacemaker during a period of instability and chaos when the world will be clamoring for peace and he will preach peace to all nations. Zechariah 9:10 says: *"...He shall speak peace to the nations; his dominion shall be 'from sea to sea, and from the River to the ends of the earth."* He will be a charismatic leader that will be brilliant in political, economic, and military power on a scale never before seen in human history and he will temporarily save the world from its desperate economic, military, and political problems. He will make a peace treaty — a covenant with Israel guaranteeing its security but it will be a false one and He will break his peace treaty with Israel after three and a half years. He will also perform counterfeit miracles that will mislead many. His ways will all be enormous lies and deceptions that will come from the works of Satan. The Scriptures clearly point it out in 2 Thessalonians 2:9-10: *"The coming of the lawless one is according to the working of Satan, with all power, signs, and lying wonders, and with all unrighteous deception among those who perish, because they did not receive the love of the truth, (Jesus Christ) that they might be saved."*

The Antichrist will be joined by his accomplice — a false prophet and will have the power and authority as the Antichrist. Revelation 13:11-14 says: *Then I saw another beast coming up out of the earth, and he had two horns like a lamb and spoke like a dragon. And he exercises all the authority of the first beast in his presence, and causes the earth and those who dwell in it to worship the first beast, whose deadly wound was healed. He performs great signs, so that he even makes fire come down from heaven on the earth in the sight of men. And he deceives those who dwell on the earth by those signs which he was granted to do in the sight of the beast, telling those who dwell on the earth to make an image to the beast who was wounded by the sword and lived.* In the above scripture of Revelations 13:11-14 the beast that comes out of the earth and has two horns and speaks like a dragon is the false prophet. He will accompany the Antichrist in helping Him to preach false peace and perform counterfeit miracles in order to win people over. The other beast that will be wounded stated in the above scripture is the Antichrist. This scripture states that the Antichrist will be assassinated at some point in his reign but will be brought back by the power of Satan. Revelation 13:12 says: "...*whose deadly wound was healed.*" This is a satanic false parallel to the resurrection of Christ, and the satanic resurrection will deceive those who have not studied the Bible and have not put their faith in our Lord Jesus Christ.

The Antichrist will use everything that God disapproves of to mislead those who are dying (the unbelievers of Jesus Christ), those who refused to love the truth that would save them — Jesus Christ. Once again, many will think that the Antichrist is the messiah because of the peace that he brings and the miracles that he performs, but they will sadly be deceived. Christ says in Matthew 24:5: *And Jesus answered and said to them: "Take heed that no one deceives you. For many will come in My name, saying, 'I am the Christ,' and will deceive many.* Matthew 24:24 says: *"For false christs and false prophets will rise and show great signs and wonders to deceive, if possible, even the elect."* In the latter point of the tribulation, the Antichrist will finally reveal his true identity by all of his blasphemies. After he and the false prophet have won people over and have made them feel secure, they will turn on them. Daniel 8:25 says: *"Through his cunning he shall cause deceit to prosper under his rule; and he shall exalt himself in his heart. He shall destroy many in their prosperity.*

Let us not fall into another one of Satan's great deceptions due to the fact of the peace we so desperately desire, and believe that this false savior — the Antichrist is the answer to our problems. He will accomplish peace where no one else has been able to before — in the Middle East, and the world will be amazed at the accomplishments of this man, but let us not be fooled. We need to know the Bible and in turn we will know of the end time scenario. We will not be fooled and know that our only true Savior is Jesus Christ. Only Christ is the answer to true lasting peace and the answer to all our dilemmas — not the Antichrist. Having faith in Christ will keep us from being deceived by ourselves, by Satan, the Antichrist, and any false prophets. It will be the difference between enjoying eternal life and suffering eternal damnation.

There have already been talks in the past about the one world government and the new world order and they are frequently happening now. It has been a long time in the making and its pieces are falling into place. This is not a fairy tale but a real world reality. The evidence is everywhere and it is also made clear in God's Word (the Bible) in what is now beginning to take place. We need to wake up and see what is happening around us. We need to compare the current events with the scriptures and you will see that the Bible is precise. World leaders, the elite and globalists are convincing the nations of the world that the only way to lasting world peace is the establishment of a new world order; and it is not being done to benefit the world, it is to benefit themselves. Socialism will not work and we should not buy into that. We need to stand up for our rights. Evil prevails when good people do nothing. The stage for the rise of the Antichrist is also being set. Without these leaders realizing it, Satan is using them to lay his groundwork for him because a one global government is an ideal environment for the Antichrist to rule.

There have also been talks about a computer chip being implanted under the skin of mankind. It will most likely be placed on the back of their hand or their forehead because they have said, "That is where it is best read by a scanner" and in fact it is stated in the scriptures, that a mark will be received either on people's right hand or on their forehead. All that we have to do is be scanned and it will show all of our information, such as our address, social security number, medical history, etc. Supposedly, it is to benefit us because it will protect our identity and help us in case of medical and financial emergencies. Once again, it is most certainly not for the benefit of the world. This type of chip will be used as a tracking device to control lives and the only means of buying and selling, which unquestionably in the near future will happen, and I will explain more on this topic. In one way or another, this is a way of world leaders and governments acting on their desire in wanting power and control over the world. They are being manipulated and influenced by Satan and they have no knowledge in what lies ahead because of their greed. Their hunger for power and control will bring forth a dictator that will rise out of these developing events. It will be the kind of dictator that made all past ones seem as if they did not even exist. Their continued ignorance, irresponsibility, greed and corruption is setting the stage and prepping the world for the most terrible and the most evil of times ever in human history! It seems that mankind has never learned anything from history and the Bible is proof.

The attempt to pass some sort of mandatory identification system upon the American public is growing rapidly, especially with the growth of technology. The public has been resisting these efforts, but government and financial agencies seem determined to implement them anyhow. This enumeration effort that is to be implemented on or in the skin of humans is already taking place worldwide. The increasing effort of worldwide implementation of chips as identification devices is accelerating rapidly. In fact these identification and tracking devices are now and have been going through experimental and developmental phases. The way things are coming along the world is most certainly headed toward a new world order.

As I have mentioned earlier, the stage for the rise of the Antichrist and his control over the world and the most terrible of times ever in human history is being set. When the Antichrist comes forth he is going to use the chip as the only means of buying and selling in the new global government. Without the chip you will not be able to buy groceries or any other necessities and you will not be able to sell anything without it as well. Basically, you will not be able to do anything without it. Revelation 13:16-17 says: *"...and that no one may buy or sell except one who has the mark or the name of the beast, or the number of his name.* We will be scanned the same way that supermarkets scan our groceries and it will be as if we are slaves. In all actuality, this chip will be the mark of the beast. It will be Satan's way of labeling his followers. In addition, there will be no more privacy because it will also be a way for the Antichrist to control millions of lives. Many will constantly be tracked and he will know where you are at all times. At the time of the Antichrist everything we take for granted now — food, water, clothes, work, and so on will be hard to come by.

During this period God will harden the hearts of the people that will refuse to love the truth that would save them — Jesus Christ. He will grant their wish of their constant unbelief of Jesus Christ and will send them strong delusions so they will believe the continuous lies of the Antichrist. 2 Thessalonians 2:11-12 says: *And for this reason God will send them strong delusion, that they should believe the lie, that they all may be condemned who did not believe the truth but had pleasure in unrighteousness.* Horrible painful sores will come upon these people who refuse to love the truth and that accept the chip (the mark of the beast) and worship the Antichrist. Revelation 16:1-3 says: *Then I heard a loud voice from the temple saying to the seven angels, "Go and pour out the bowls of the wrath of God on the earth." So the first went and poured out his bowl upon the earth, and a foul and loathsome sore came upon the men who had the mark of the beast and those who worshiped his image.* The Antichrist will cause all walks of life to receive the mark of the beast and they will receive it willingly. But many will accept Christ and under no circumstance will they receive the mark, even when being forced to take it under the threat of death. They will rather lose their life than their soul because it is much better to do so, for the reason that the Lord will raise them up in a new glorified body. They will forever be saved and will never suffer eternal damnation because they will have turned to Christ. The people that accept the chip from the

Antichrist, which will be put on their right hand or forehead, will mean that they have pledged their allegiance to Him and will have sold their soul to Satan. They have chosen Satan to be their eternal master and have sealed their fate and will be eternally doomed. The wrath of God will come upon these followers of Satan that refused to love the truth that would save them — Jesus Christ. They will be tormented day and night, burning in the lake of fire forever. Revelation 13:16 says: *"He causes all, both small and great, rich and poor, free and slave, to receive a mark on their right hand or on their foreheads."* Revelation 14:9-11 says: *"Then a third angel followed them, saying with a loud voice, 'If anyone worships the beast and his image, and receives his mark on his forehead or on his hand, he himself shall also drink of the wine of the wrath of God, which is poured out full strength into the cup of His indignation. He shall be tormented with fire and brimstone in the presence of the holy angels and in the presence of the Lamb. And the smoke of their torment ascends forever and ever; and they have no rest day or night, who worship the beast and his image, and whoever receives the mark of his name."*

Satan is very intelligent in implementing his schemes and he is good in getting people to swallow his bait. Be very vigilant in these changing times of technology. Satan can use different means in getting you to swallow his bait (the mark of the beast). The mark may not necessarily be a chip that is implemented; it could be anything, perhaps it may be a bar code that will be tattooed on a person that mankind may rather use instead of the chip. But in any case, it still will be a tracking device and the only way to buy and sell, and as I have stated earlier, in all actuality it will be Satan's way in marking his followers and their eternal death. It is the mark of the beast and it is now being put into effect and becoming a reality.

Moving forward, God will send out 144,000 servants from the twelve tribes of Israel to preach His word to help others that are not saved, come to Jesus Christ during this period. These 144,000 servants will be sealed with the seal of God on their foreheads so they cannot be harmed by God's judgments. Revelation 7:3-4 says: *"Do not harm the land or the sea or the trees until we put a seal on the foreheads of the servants of our God." Then I heard the number of those who were sealed: 144,000 from all the tribes of Israel."* By the grace of God many will come to accept Christ because of the preaching of these 144.000 servants of God and will be forgiven.

God will also send two prophets and give them great power to accomplish His Will as well. The two prophets will inflict much misery and the purpose of all the misery that these two prophets inflict on the earth, is to turn people to God in repentance. These two men will also proclaim the gospel and provide hope for those that are lost. Their message will be for the salvation of people's souls. They will have no message as to how you can avoid the hell that life on earth has become but you will have the hope of eternal salvation. When they finish their testimony and complete God's work then God will allow the two prophets to be killed by the Antichrist. The misery that the two prophets inflict will be so great that when the Antichrist does finally kill these two, the world believing that the two prophets of God were evil, will rejoice and the world will be in for a rude awakening. The bodies of the two prophets will remain in the streets of Jerusalem for three and one half days for the world to see. These two prophets of God will then be resurrected from the dead by the Lord in the sight of all who are watching, via television etc. and they will rise up into the heavens. This event will validate the Antichrist as being a false messiah and it will open many eyes. The Bible says that great fear will fall on those who have witnessed this event. In that same hour God will cause a great earthquake. Many will die and many will be afraid and will give God glory for what they have seen and witnessed. Revelations 11:3 says: *"And I will give power to my two witnesses, and they will prophesy one thousand two hundred and sixty days, clothed in sackcloth."* Revelations 11:7-13 says: *"When they finish their testimony, the beast that ascends out of the bottomless pit will make war against them, overcome them, and kill them. And their dead bodies will lie in the street of the great city which spiritually is called Sodom and Egypt, where also our Lord was crucified. Then those from the peoples, tribes, tongues, and nations will see their dead bodies three-and-a-half days, and not allow their dead bodies to be put into graves. And those who dwell on the earth will rejoice over them, make merry, and send gifts to one another, because these two prophets tormented those who dwell on the earth. Now after the three-and-a-half days the breath of life from God entered them, and they stood on their feet, and great fear fell on those who saw them. And they heard a loud voice from heaven saying to them, "Come up here." And they ascended to heaven in a cloud, and their enemies saw them. In the same hour there was a great earthquake, and a tenth of the city fell. In the earthquake seven thousand people were killed, and the rest were afraid and gave glory to the God of heaven.*

Many of God's elect by faith, will be provided for by God and will persevere through this great time of suffering and be saved when Jesus comes back to save them during His second coming. (The elect are all the people that will come to accept Jesus Christ during the great tribulation period and the ones who will refuse to worship the Antichrist and refuse the mark of the beast). Matthew 24:13 says: *"But he who endures to the end shall be saved."* On the other hand, many of Christ's other elect will pay for their newly found faith and will suffer greatly at the hands of the Antichrist. The Antichrist will not like the idea of people accepting Jesus Christ and will launch a brutal persecution and will kill those who will reject the mark of the beast and who testify on Jesus' behalf and for the Word of God. Revelation 13:15 says: *"He was granted power to give breath to the image of the beast, that the image of the beast should both speak and cause as many as would not worship the image of the beast to be killed."* Daniel 8:24 says: *"His power shall be mighty, but not by his own power; he shall destroy fearfully, and shall prosper and thrive; he shall destroy the mighty, and also the holy people."*

In the great tribulation there will be famine, plague, the deceit and persecution of the Antichrist, wars, and God's righteous wrath will be poured out upon on earth and so on. It will be so bad that God will have to shorten those days for the sake of His elect. Christ will have to intervene, which is His second coming in order to stop the persecution and to prevent complete genocide of His elect. Once again, the elect are all the people that will come to accept Jesus Christ during this period of great tribulation. Matthew 24:22 says: *"And unless those days were shortened, no flesh would be saved; but for the elect's sake those days will be shortened."*

Continuing on, the Antichrist will set Himself up in God's new rebuilt temple in Jerusalem and proclaim to be God. 2 Thessalonians 2:4 says: *"...who opposes and exalts himself above all that is called God or that is worshiped, so that he sits as God in the temple of God, showing himself that he is God."* He will defile the temple and abolish the daily sacrifice which in the scriptures is known as the abomination of desolation. Daniel 11:31 says: *"...And forces[1] shall be mustered by him, and they shall defile the sanctuary fortress; then they shall take away the daily sacrifices, and place there the abomination of desolation."* At that point the Israelites who have not received the chip (the mark of the beast) will open their eyes and see that the Antichrist is a false messiah by all of his blasphemies and the fact that he will defile God's temple and abolish the daily sacrifice. They will then know they have been deceived and they will come to realize that our true Messiah came two thousand years ago — Jesus Christ, and will run off to the mountains for safety. Matthew 24:15-16 says: *"Therefore when you see the 'abomination of desolation,' spoken of by Daniel the prophet, standing in the holy place"* (whoever reads, let him understand), *"then let those who are in Judea flee to the mountains."* The Lord will have a place prepared for these people and God will provide for them exactly as He did when the Israelites journeyed to the Promised Land.

Toward the end of the great tribulation, the Antichrist will plunge the armies of the world into a series of wars involving a number of devastating battles that lead to the cataclysmic battle of Armageddon. He will lead mankind the brink of distinction, which will cause Christ to descend from heaven and intervene — the second coming of Jesus Christ. The Antichrist will gather his armies in Armageddon where Christ will be and wage war against Him. Revelations 16:16 says: *"And they gathered them together to the place called in Hebrew, Armageddon."* Revelations 19:19 says: *"And I*

saw the beast, the kings of the earth, and their armies, gathered together to make war against Him who sat on the horse
(Jesus Christ) and against His army." In a futile attempt
to defeat Christ, the Antichrist and His armies will be terribly defeated. Jesus will finally bring His ultimate judgment
upon the Antichrist and the false prophet and He will immediately throw them both alive in the lake of fire. The rest of
the armies will be destroyed by simply speaking them out of
existence. Revelation 19:20-21 says: *"Then the beast was
captured, and with him the false prophet who worked signs
in his presence, by which he deceived those who received the
mark of the beast and those who worshiped his image. These
two were cast alive into the lake of fire burning with brimstone. And the rest were killed with the sword which proceeded from the mouth of Him who sat on the horse (Jesus
Christ). And all the birds were filled with their flesh."*

The prophecy does not end there. Satan himself will
also be doomed but will have a different fate. He will be
cast into a bottomless pit and he will be chained and bound
for a thousand years. The bottomless pit will be closed and
sealed above him, so that he should no longer lead astray
and deceive the nations when Christ brings in His Kingdom.

Then judgment will come upon all that are still living and all that are dead!

Christ will bring in peace and righteousness and will establish His Kingdom on earth and all who have accepted Jesus Christ will reign and live with Him. Revelation 20:2-4 says: *"He laid hold of the dragon, that serpent of old, who is the Devil and Satan, and bound him for a thousand years; and he cast him into the bottomless pit, and shut him up, and set a seal on him, so that he should deceive the nations no more till the thousand years were finished. But after these things he must be released for a little while. And I saw thrones, and they sat on them, and judgment was committed to them. Then I saw the souls of those who had been beheaded for their witness to Jesus and for the word of God, who had not worshiped the beast or his image, and had not received his mark on their foreheads or on their hands. And they lived and reigned with Christ for a thousand years."* After the thousand years are up Satan must be liberated from his prison for a short time. He will once again deceive nations, but this time he will be done for good and will immediately be hurled into the fiery lake of fire where the Antichrist and the false prophet are and they will be tormented day and night forever and ever. Revelation 20:10 says: *"The devil, who* deceived them, was cast into the lake of fire and brimstone where the beast and the false prophet are. And they will be tormented day and night forever and ever." The old world will then be destroyed and a new heaven and earth will be established and there will be everlasting peace. Revelation 21:1-3 says: *"Now I saw a new heaven and a new earth, for the first heaven and the first earth had passed away. Also there was no more sea. Then I, John, saw the holy city, New Jerusalem, coming down out of heaven from God, prepared as a bride adorned for her husband. And I heard a loud voice from heaven saying, "Behold, the tabernacle of God is with men, and He will dwell with them, and they shall be His people. God Himself will be with them and be their God."*

Once again, I encourage you to turn to Jesus Christ immediately and find refuge in Him and in the Word of God before it is too late, for we do not know when the hour of our death will be and also by the grace of God that we who are still on earth will be raptured and taken by the Lord before the horrific period of tribulation takes place.

What will the end time great tribulation be like? Will God unleash His fury upon the world at that point in time?

The great tribulation will be far worse than any human can ever imagine! Matthew 24:21 says: *"For then shall be great tribulation, such as was not since the beginning of the world to this time, no, nor ever shall be."* Not only will the Antichrist reign during this time as I have mentioned earlier and deceive many and also launch a brutal execution and behead all who refuse to worship him as God, as well as also plunging the armies of the world into a series of wars involving a number of devastating battles that lead to the cataclysmic battle of Armageddon, but the righteous wrath of God will begin to be relentlessly poured out on all unrighteousness at that point as well. There will be a great deal of plague, pestilences, famine and disease in the world at this time, and by far worse than anything we are experiencing now and have ever experienced! We will no longer be living in the age of grace. God's judgments will start out with hail being mixed with blood and will begin to fall from the sky upon people and a third of the earth will be burned up. Revelation 8:7 says: *The first angel sounded: And hail and fire followed, mingled with blood, and they were thrown to the earth. And a third of the trees were burned up, and all green grass was burned up.* Revelation 16:21 says: *"And great hail from heaven fell upon men, each hailstone about the weight of a talent (approximately 125 pounds). Men blasphemed God because of the plague of the hail, since that plague was exceedingly great."* A huge mountain all ablaze will be thrown into the sea. A third of the sea will turn into blood, a third of the living creatures in the sea will die and a third of the ships will be destroyed. Revelation 8:8-9 says: *The second angel sounded his trumpet, and something like a huge mountain, all ablaze, was thrown into the sea. A third of the sea turned into blood, a third of the living creatures in the sea died, and a third of the ships were destroyed.* Revelation 16:3-4 says: *Then the second angel poured out his bowl on the sea, and it became blood as of a dead man; and every living creature in the sea died. Then the third angel poured out his bowl on the rivers and springs of water, and they became blood.* An asteroid or a meteor will fall to the earth and a third of the waters will turn bitter and many will die from drinking it. Revelation 8:10-11 says: *The third angel sounded his trumpet, and a great star, blazing like a torch, fell from the sky on a third of the rivers and on* the springs of water—the name of the star is Wormwood. A third of the waters turned bitter, and many people died from the waters that had become bitter. The moon and the sun will be darkened and day will become night. Revelation 8:12 says: *The fourth angel sounded his trumpet, and a third of the sun was struck, a third of the moon, and a third of the stars, so that a third of them turned dark. A third of the day was without light, and also a third of the night.* There will be a great worldwide earthquake leveling every mountain into the sea and so on. Revelation 16:18 says: *"And there were noises and thunderings and lightnings; and there was a great earthquake, such a mighty and great earthquake as had not occurred since men were on the earth."* People will faint because they will be overwhelmed with terror. Man's heart will fail from fear. Luke 21:26 says: *"...men's hearts failing them from fear and the expectation of those things which are coming on the earth, for the powers of the heavens will be shaken.*

It will be extremely unimaginable what people on earth will observe during this time. They will be in for a rude awakening. It will be just like the days of Noah when the flood came. No one believed that it would happen and there-fore, were all swept away. It will be a time of much chaos, carnage and destruction. One third of the population will die and unfortunately many without ever wanting anything to do with our Lord God and His Son Jesus Christ.

It seems that we neglect our souls. Should we not be putting as much time and effort in our spiritual being and worrying about eternal life, rather than putting all our time and effort in our physical being and worrying about the things of this world?

Absolutely! But sadly, many would rather trade their soul, in exchange for worldly desires. We give much attention to our physical life that we have nothing left to give for the life that is eternal. We are living in an unsaved way. We should not be obsessed with this life and worry about gain because we cannot take it with us when we pass. 1 Timothy 6:7 says: *"For we brought nothing into this world, and it is certain we can carry nothing out."* We need to seek the Kingdom of God and everything else that we need will be given to us. God is of the spirit and therefore, the only way to gain everlasting life is for us to be of the spirit and not of the flesh. We are not on this planet to obtain glory, make money, have careers, and then die. We are on this planet to fulfill God's purpose and by His grace receive eternal salvation. We spend way too much time trying to bring our bodies and our lives to perfection when we should be exercising more time on our spiritual being; it is much more important.

John 6:63 says: *"It is the Spirit who gives life; the flesh profits nothing. The words that I speak to you are spirit, and they are life."* Things of this world pass away and our soul is eternal. Our physical body is just a temporary means to carry our soul until our bodies die. Our whole lives we have been molded and deceived into just believing in what we see and instead it is faith that we need to be relying on. Many do not give much thought of the afterlife until someone close to them dies. It only makes sense to think that there is an afterlife. Why bother going through the course of living just to go nowhere? It seems like a great deal of trouble to go through for nothing.

We should take care of our physical being too, but we should not give it more attention than it needs, only enough to sustain it. God wants us to provide just enough for ourselves to get through this life and we should count our blessings and be happy with what we have. 1 Timothy 6:8 says: *"...And having food and clothing, with these we shall be content."* Do not worry; once we put our trust in God He will not leave us on our own. He will get us through this life and fill our needs. Hebrews 13:5 says: *"Let your conduct be without covetousness (greed); be content with such things as you have. For He Himself has said, 'I will never leave you nor forsake you.' "* Our focus needs to be on our soul and we need to give it all our attention because the soul is the essence of our being. It is what moves on after this life has passed. It will either live on forever or it will be destined for eternal damnation. Once again it all depends on our actions while we are on earth. It is much better to lose your life than it is your soul. Putting the spirit first will also make you to be a more compassionate, considerate, loving, and an unselfish person. Use your good judgments that God has given you, receive Christ and partake in God's amazing spiritual world. Whatever we have to do in this life to obtain eternal life is certainly worth it, and the only way to obtain eternal life is to let go of this physical one. We have to be willing to turn our back on all this world offers because this life is only temporal and it will soon pass. Therefore, we need to store up our treasures in heaven and let go of our fleshly desires. Matthew 6:19-21 says: *"Do not lay up for yourselves treasures on earth, where moth and rust destroy and where thieves break in and steal; but lay up for yourselves treasures in heaven, where neither moth nor rust destroys and where thieves do not break in and steal. For where your treasure is, there your heart will be also."*

We are driven by the things and the principles of this world, the works of our flesh, and Satan. We have to fight and stand strong against them. These are our enemies and they will keep us from knowing Christ and will constantly keep us busy with sin and unrighteousness. We need to invest in what has eternal value and not invest in our sinful temporary satisfaction. Do not be focused on a life that cannot be kept, but focus on a life that can be — eternal life (the soul). Luke 9:23-24 says: *"Then He said to them all, 'If anyone desires to come after Me, let him deny himself, and take up his cross daily, and follow Me. For whoever desires to save his life will lose it, but whoever loses his life for My sake will save it.' "* We waste much time worrying about our temporal life on this earth when the true things in life are free and eternal. We need to seek the wealth, splendor and wisdom that are stored up in Jesus Christ. Anything that is done outside the will of God and outside of the spirit, He considers it wasted time. Mark 8:36 says: *"For what will it profit a man if he gains the whole world, and loses his own soul?"* We need to have an eternal and spiritual mindset and stop being molded into the world's form, so let the Spirit of God transform you. When we follow Gods ways, <u>WE WILL</u> be victorious, both physically and eternally. The value of having God the Father and His Son Jesus Christ in our lives is worth much more than any earthly treasure. Spiritual joys are much better than any worldly joys. We should be using this time on earth to seek out God's perfect Will and walk in the spirit rather than fulfilling the sinful lust of our flesh. Galatians 5:19-21 says: *"Now the works of the flesh are evident, which are: adultery, fornication, uncleanness, lewdness, idolatry, sorcery, hatred, contentions, jealousies, outbursts of wrath, selfish ambitions, dissensions, heresies, envy, murders, drunkenness, revelries, and the like; of which I tell you beforehand, just as I also told you in time past, that those who practice such things will not inherit the kingdom of God."* The works of the flesh will keep us from inheriting the Kingdom of God and lead us to our eternal death.

We need to seek out spiritual knowledge rather than worldly knowledge. We cannot understand God's Will and our spiritual gifts that He has given us all, if we continue to walk in the flesh and not in the spirit. But not only that, it is God and only God that can save us from all of the lies and deceptions that will eventually lead to our eternal destruction if we do not wake up and seek Him out! Walking by faith will require obedience to God and it may take some hard work to live by His standards but it is far from impossible. What we have to give up in this life is nothing compared to all that we will inherit, including a joyous eternal life with God our Father and His Son Jesus Christ. If we prevail over this world — our fleshly desires, we will inherit all things that God promises in His Word (the Bible), incredibly and above all we will have the right to be one of His children as well. Revelations 21:7 says: *"He who overcomes shall inherit all things, and I will be his God and he shall be My son."*

The longer you wait to come to faith in Christ, the more you will let this world shape your life and as a result, the harder it will be for you to leave your fleshly pleasures and desires behind you and receive Christ! Do not be hardened to the truth, but rather bow down in faith at the feet of our risen Lord and Savior and tell Him that you will receive Him at this present moment. I encourage you to do so <u>NOW</u> for your sake, your families sake, and Jesus' sake before it is eternally too late!

In conclusion

I f anyone feels that they have been offended by this book in any way, please do not be. Let me ask you, would you rather have a friend who cares and tells you the truth so that you can be aware of the things that are going on around you that you are not aware of? Or would you rather have a friend putting you in harm's way by telling you lies and letting you hear everything that they want you to hear and what you want to hear? The truth may hurt at times, but it is the truth that sets us free! It is God's moral law that frees us from all the burdens of man's self-rule and bondage that originates from Satan! God will condemn us as individuals and as a nation as well if we continue to practice immorality. We need to pray for God's protection and intervention and we need to exercise faith in Jesus Christ!

This is not a mystery; the Bible spells everything out for us clearly and in great detail. There would be true enlightenment and we would gain great knowledge and wisdom if we would just take the time to turn to the Bible. We would understand that these are not the words of a mere man but these are the Words of the living Almighty God!

Respect for God, His creation, and His Holy Word is the only way we will ever find true freedom. The blood of Jesus Christ that was shed for mankind is enough to heal the world. It is not too late to repent and turn our hearts to Christ. We can bring healing and life to this land that we love if we will humble ourselves before God almighty. 2 Chronicles 7:14 says: *"…if My people who are called by My name will humble themselves, and pray and seek My face, and turn from their wicked ways, then I will hear from heaven, and will forgive their sin and heal their land."*

We need to open our eyes and our hearts to Him and we will see how good God really is. We must stop taking Him out of everything because it is He who wants nothing but the best for us and to help us dearly. Remember, we as God's children have forsaken Him in many ways of blocking out His existence. God on the other hand loves us all as He always has and as He always will. He has given us free will and He pleads with us to use our free will wisely. We must return to prayer and put our faith in Jesus Christ and let us not forsake Him. Remember Sodom and Gomorra? Many of us have closed our hearts to what is right in order to live for our own evil lustful desires. We must wake up and stop being deceived by Satan and his evil deceptions.

God did not send His Son Jesus into the world to condemn us, but He sent Him into the world in order to save us. John 3:17 says: *"For God did not send His Son into the world to condemn the world, but that the world through Him might be saved."* God wants us to experience His love, fullness, and glory and most importantly to save us from our sins because He knows how terrible hell is and He does not wish any of His children to perish in eternal damnation.

Sadly, we shut Him out and we do not allow ourselves the chance to experience His love. We are only hurting and deceiving ourselves by not giving Jesus Christ an opportunity to come into our lives. Do not be blind to the existence of God, rather be willing to search Him out for yourselves. There is NOTHING more worth our while and NOTHING more important than to seek out God, and there is NOTHING more precious than God Himself. We should love the Lord our God with all our heart, with all our soul, with all our mind and with all our strength.

I pray that we recognize that truth and are willing to change our ways and come to Jesus Christ before it is too late. Have faith in Christ that He will lead you in the life that He has planned for you and let your faith be accompanied by action, for without action faith is dead. Having genuine faith in Jesus Christ will enlighten you in your journey in life and will also give you true life after death.

In the long run, we must all face physical death so why face eternal damnation (hell) when we have the opportunity to accept God's free gift to us and experience a joyous everlasting life?

Willingly receive Christ in your life, repent of your sins, and by the grace of God, eternal salvation will be given to you. For in Jesus Christ we find life. Proverbs 8:35 says: *"For whoever finds me finds life, and obtains favor from the LORD."*

The value of having God the Father and His Son Jesus Christ in our lives is priceless! It is worth much more than any earthly treasure! When will we come to realize that we are in need of the Lord in every aspect of our lives and learn not to trust in our own ways anymore?! The one most important and biggest thing in the world is <u>FAITH</u>! You will be surprised what faith can do!

Prayer for Salvation

If you have never accepted Christ as your personal Lord and Savior and I strongly encourage you to do so, you need to first let God give you a spiritual rebirth by repenting of your sins because sin separates us from God and hinders the spirit. John 3:3 says: *Jesus answered and said to him, "Most assuredly, I say to you, unless one is born again, he cannot see the kingdom of God."* 1 John 1:9 says: *"If we confess our sins, He is faithful and just to forgive us our sins and to cleanse us from all unrighteousness."* We need a new nature — a divine holy nature, because we cannot truly be good due to our fleshly sinful nature and because of our fleshly desires. Therefore, we cannot be forgiven and gain salvation, and be children of God if we desire the worldly pleasures rather than the pleasures of the spirit. Once we receive Christ, God will forgive us of our sins and will transform us and give us our new holy nature. We will then be Christ-like and be children of God and will have gained everlasting life. We will be living and enjoying the spirit filled life and no longer of the flesh that causes us to live in sin, which leads to hopelessness and misery and eventually eternal separation from God. Jesus Christ did all the work on the cross and all that you have to do to accept Christ and be forgiven is to sincerely pray a simple prayer with faith. By the good grace of God He will then forgive you and awaken you spiritually and you will be given His free gift of eternal salvation. Heaven is a holy place and we cannot enter it until we have asked Christ to cleanse us of our sins and have been given a holy nature by God through the spiritual rebirth.

Pray

Dear Heavenly Father please forgive me for I have sinned. I'm a sinner that needs salvation. I turn from my sins and my selfish ways to live my new life in Christ. Thank You for sending your Son to die on the cross for my sins. I also believe that He rose again and now He lives. I choose to have your Son, Jesus Christ to live His life in me and through me. I surrender all that I am, all that I have, and all I shall be to you, and help me to seek out Your Will. Make me the person that You always wanted me to be. Thank you for saving me. In Jesus' name I pray. Amen!

If you have prayed this prayer in faith, you have opened the door for the Spirit of God to come into your life and change your sinful heart and you have gained eternal salvation. Faith in Jesus Christ is the key that unlocks the door to the power and to the grace of God!

There is <u>MUCH HOPE</u> with Jesus Christ! Repenting of your sins, praying with the right motives, persevering in prayer, and having faith, Jesus Heals!

Poem

When You Ask Me

When you ask Me to lead you through your journey and take control of your life, trust in Me and I will take you by the hand and guide you on the right path and steer you through your trials and tribulations.

When you ask Me to come into your life and heal your soul and mend your broken heart, I will hold you tightly in My arms and comfort you with all of my love. Through Me there is much hope and I will fill you with My Holy Spirit and bless you with a great deal of peace and joy.

*When you ask Me to help you make decisions in your life,
listen closely and I will help you through someone or something find the answer you are looking for and the right
answer you sought out by asking Me will be felt within you.*

*When you ask Me to remove all of your burdens from your
life, cast all of your cares upon Me and I will put everything on My shoulders and carry you through
all your pain and suffering.*

*When you ask Me to do My Will, stay with Me in true faith,
through thick and thin and I will show you the life and the
blessings that I have intended for you.*

*When you ask Me for strength and courage,
I will lift you up with wings as eagles and make it easier for
you to attain your purpose in life.*

*When you ask Me to protect you from all evil including
your enemies, I will be there watching over you day and
night and I will not once take My eyes off of you and let
anything or anyone cause any harm to you.*

When you ask Me for My wisdom, which is worth more than any earthly treasure, I will enlighten you with the light of My Word and open your eyes to the divine truth.

Please ask Me my precious child. Seek Me and give Me a chance to come into your life. Knock and the door will be opened to you. I wait day and night just to hear from you. I love you more than you can ever imagine. Please ask Me and I will truly listen. I your Father from above, will give you My blessings and My eternal heavenly kingdom.

Written by
Jesus Christ
through
robert s. russo

Proverbs of Wisdom

"The fear of the LORD is the beginning of knowledge, but fools despise wisdom and instruction."

Proverbs 1:7

"Happy is the man who finds wisdom, And the man who gains understanding; For her proceeds are better than the profits of silver, And her gain than fine gold."

Proverbs 3:13-14

"The LORD by wisdom founded the earth; By understanding He established the heavens."

Proverbs 3:19

"Get wisdom! Get understanding! Do not forget, nor turn away from the words of my mouth. Do not forsake her, and she will preserve you; Love her, and she will keep you."

Proverbs 4:5-6

"Wisdom is the principal thing; Therefore get wisdom. And in all your getting, get understanding."

Proverbs 4:7

"I have taught you in the way of wisdom; I have led you in right paths."

Proverbs 4:11

"My son, pay attention to my wisdom; Lend your ear to my understanding, That you may preserve discretion, And your lips may keep knowledge."

Proverbs 5:1-2

"For wisdom is better than rubies, And all the things one may desire cannot be compared with her."

Proverbs 8:11

"For whoever finds me finds life, and obtains favor from the LORD."

Proverbs 8:35

"But he who sins against Me wrongs his own soul; all those who hate Me love death."

Proverbs 8:36

"The fear of the LORD is the beginning of wisdom, And the knowledge of the Holy One is understanding."

Proverbs 9:10

"The lips of the righteous feed many, but fools die for lack of wisdom."

Proverbs 10:21

"To do evil is like sport to a fool, but a man of understanding has wisdom."

Proverbs 10:23

"When the whirlwind passes by, the wicked is no more, but the righteous has an everlasting foundation."

Proverbs 10:25

"The mouth of the righteous brings forth wisdom, But the perverse tongue will be cut out."

> *Proverbs 10:31*

"When pride comes, then comes shame; But with the humble is wisdom."

> *Proverbs 11:2*

"Though they join forces, the wicked will not go unpunished; but the posterity of the righteous will be delivered."

> *Proverbs 11:21*

"The fruit of the righteous is a tree of life, and he who wins souls is wise."

> *Proverbs 11:30*

"The way of a fool is right in his own eyes, but he who heeds counsel is wise."

> *Proverbs 12:15*

"A scoffer seeks wisdom and does not find it, But knowledge is easy to him who understands."

Proverbs 14:6

"The fear of the LORD is the instruction of wisdom, And before honor is humility."

Proverbs 15:33

"How much better to get wisdom than gold! And to get understanding is to be chosen rather than silver."

Proverbs 16:16

"Understanding is a wellspring of life to him who has it. But the correction of fools is folly."

Proverbs 16:22

"Why is there in the hand of a fool the purchase price of wisdom, since he has no heart for it?"

Proverbs 17:16

"Wisdom is in the sight of him who has understanding, But the eyes of a fool are on the ends of the earth."

Proverbs 17:24

Even a fool is counted wise when he holds his peace;
When he shuts his lips, he is considered perceptive.

Proverbs 17:28

"He who gets wisdom loves his own soul; He who keeps understanding will find good."

Proverbs 19:8

"He who follows righteousness and mercy finds life, righteousness, and honor."

Proverbs 21:21

"There is no wisdom or understanding or counsel against the LORD."

Proverbs 21:30

"Do not overwork to be rich; Because of your own understanding, cease!"

Proverbs 23:4

"Do not speak in the hearing of a fool, For he will despise the wisdom of your words."

Proverbs 23:9

"Hear, my son, and be wise; and guide your heart in the way."

Proverbs 23:19

"Buy the truth, and do not sell it, Also wisdom and instruction and understanding."

Proverbs 23:23

"Through wisdom a house is built, And by understanding it is established; By knowledge the rooms are filled with all precious and pleasant riches. A wise man is strong, Yes, a man of knowledge increases strength; For by wise counsel you will wage your own war, And in a multitude of counselors there is safety.

Proverbs 24:3-6

"So shall the knowledge of wisdom be to your soul; If you have found it, there is a prospect, And your hope will not be cut off."

Proverbs 24:14

"For there will be no prospect for the evil man; the lamp of the wicked will be put out."

Proverbs 24:20

"Happy is the man who is always reverent, but he who hardens his heart will fall into calamity."

Proverbs 28:14

"He who trusts in his own heart is a fool, but whoever walks wisely will be delivered."

Proverbs 28:26

"Whoever loves wisdom makes his father rejoice, But a companion of harlots wastes his wealth."

Proverbs 29:3

Bibliography

Answers, Campus Crusade for Christ, Inc., First Tyndale House Publisher, Inc. (1980).

Bible.com Ministries, Bible.com, Inc., www.bible.com (1995-2005).

Christ Centered Evangelism, Barbieri, Jeff (2009).

Fall in Love with the God Jesus Knows, Hopler, Whitney, InterVarsity Press (2009).

Hell, Wiese, Bill, Charisma House (2008).

In Touch Ministries, Stanley, Charles Dr., www.intouch.org (2010).

Is There a God?, Adamson, Marilyn, www.everystudent.com.

Media Ministries, Lindsey, Hal, www.hallindsey.com (2010).

Questions Ministries, www.gotquestions.org (2002-2010).

THE OCCULT – What does the Bible say about it?, Paul S. Taylor, www.christiananswers.net (1995-2010).

The rapture: What you need to know, Mickey, Michael G., www.rapturealert.com (2008).

THE SECRET KINGDOM, Robertson, Pat, The Christian Broadcasting Network Inc., www.CBN.com *(2010).*

Tomorrow's World, www.tomorrowsworld.org (2009).

Truth for life, Begg, Alistair, www.truthforlife.org (2009).

Breinigsville, PA USA
15 October 2010
247305BV00009B/1/P